THE BREAKUP BOOK

"I knew this significant and original book would be informative—and it is, very. What I didn't expect: pure inspiration in a fresh voice that will make readers feel they have a smart and sassy new best friend. Surviving a broken heart is not easy, yet Robins creates an environment through her writing that is comfortable, safe, and welcoming."

—**Giuliana Rancic**, Anchor, *E! News*

"I loved this book. Charismatic and engaging, Lesley approaches her readers with humor and compassion. After taking in this profound and deeply moving book, you will forever know how to mend your heart, no matter what the situation."

—**Sherry Gaba**, LCSW, Life Coach on
Celebrity Rehab with Dr. Drew

"Lesley Robins is very wise and brutally honest. It's tough out there. This book is written in a funny, straightforward, no B.S. kind of way and reminds me how delicate relationships and breakups really are."

—**Kevin Connolly**, Actor, *Entourage*

"Lesley Robins rocks and here's why: I have a beautiful, young daughter, and as a young father who knows what it's like out there in the world, what I fear most about her growing up is . . . boys. I look forward to passing on these words of wisdom to her. This book is awesome. Read it."

—**Constantine Maroulis**, *American Idol* Finalist,
Tony® Nominee, *Rock of Ages*

"With humor, authenticity, wisdom, and a style that is all her own, Lesley Robins delivers an important message, in a fresh new way, that may save millions from stewing in the depths of anguish for longer than necessary. The reader will feel they have just connected with a good friend who really knows the pain they are going through . . . and how to get to the other side. Her words are uplifting, motivational, and extremely supportive."

—**Tammi Baliszewski**, PhD, Host at Empower Radio

"Lesley charms her readers by taking a delicate subject and writing about it in a smart and witty way, like something taken right out of a *Sex and the City* episode. A modern-day relationship bible that will help mend any broken heart."

—**Carissa Chesanek**, Miami Editor, Zagat

"Every word she writes in this book hits home! Being in the midst of a breakup, I was clinging to every word. I wanted to erase some of the missteps I'd already taken and do it her way . . . it makes more sense. Lesley gives spot-on advice in every portion of her book but the section I coveted was 'Step Nine: Get Out of Dodge.' It works wonders, as does the rest of her heartfelt advice."

—**Peta Phipps**, Publisher, *Caribbean Living* magazine

THE BREAK UP BOOK

20 Steps to Heal a **BROKEN HEART**

LESLEY ROBINS

NEW YORK

THE BREAKUP BOOK
20 Steps to Heal a BROKEN HEART

Published in New York, New York, by Morgan James Publishing. Morgan James and The Entrepreneurial Publisher are trademarks of Morgan James, LLC. www.MorganJamesPublishing.com

The Morgan James Speakers Group can bring authors to your live event. For more information or to book an event visit The Morgan James Speakers Group at www.TheMorganJamesSpeakersGroup.com.

A **free** eBook edition is available with the purchase of this print book.

CLEARLY PRINT YOUR NAME ABOVE IN UPPER CASE

Instructions to claim your free eBook edition:
1. Download the BitLit app for Android or iOS
2. Write your name in **UPPER CASE** on the line
3. Use the BitLit app to submit a photo
4. Download your eBook to any device

ISBN 978-1-63047-121-7 paperback
ISBN 978-1-63047-122-4 eBook
ISBN 978-1-63047-123-1 hardcover
Library of Congress Control Number:
2014934764

Cover Design by:
Rachel Lopez
www.r2cdesign.com

Interior Design by:
Bonnie Bushman
bonnie@caboodlegraphics.com

Photo by:
Shaun Benson

In an effort to support local communities, raise awareness and funds, Morgan James Publishing donates a percentage of all book sales for the life of each book to Habitat for Humanity Peninsula and Greater Williamsburg.

Get involved today, visit
www.MorganJamesBuilds.com

Habitat for Humanity
Peninsula and
Greater Williamsburg
Building Partner

I dedicate this book to
A man that came into the world
During my darkest time
Who reminded me what joy is
My nephew, Dennis Ian,
Or as I call him,
Munchkin.

TABLE OF CONTENTS

MY BREAKUP STORY

In 2010, I went through a disastrous breakup. It was a breakup that dragged on for another year and a half, a breakup that had happened many times before with the same guy. I wrote about it. Slowly, I healed. And then, miraculously, I became awesome.

My story is nothing new. Love, unbridled passion, crushed hearts. No one has it all figured out. No one. Everything seems possible when in love. Life-changing decisions can be motivated by love; likewise, life-destroying decisions can come from the heart. I am not immune to falling flat on my face in search of this natural high and having to pick myself up piece by piece when it came crashing down in the end.

Breakups happen to everyone. They don't discriminate by race, gender, age, sexual orientation, hometown, or celebrity status. Your heart could have been busted up many times before and glued back together like Humpty Dumpty, but it will break again and test your strength. Breakups will humble you and tear you apart. Some breakups can make you feel like the world is coming to an end.

Over and over again the process goes—falling in love and finding that bliss, to the breakup you didn't want to see coming and the heartbreak that follows. That moment when one side of the seesaw comes crashing down because the other person decides to get off the ride, and there you are stuck at the bottom with no one on the other side. You start to cry. Your body aches. Why would the other person get off the seesaw? Playgrounds used to be fun. WTF?!

A breakup isn't something you can ever really prepare for, either. You may have a hunch that something is about to go down, but you never really know when that conversation will strike. Even if you do suspect a breakup is about to happen, but it's not *you* pulling the trigger, you will try to talk yourself out of believing it's about to happen. And believe it or not, most likely there is nothing you can do to stop it.

There are many kinds of breakups. There are the ones where you've been dating for a couple of weeks and you both know it's not going anywhere, so you each walk away relatively unharmed. Then there's the breakup that happens after a few months of dating, where hearts probably will be slightly broken, maybe one more than the other, but it wasn't a ton of time that you invested into the relationship, so you walk away in one piece, albeit missing that person for a while. That one takes some time to heal, and it's not fun to get over them. You may go back for more after the initial breakup, but that gets old pretty fast.

You have the not-so-mutual breakup that hurts no matter how long you've been with the person, because no matter what, rejection sucks. Being rejected in any situation isn't cool, especially when it's someone you shared time with, shared a bed with, and shared your life with. Some may even say leaving a man's place after you met him once is a breakup, but that one is debatable. It seems all men we are with, in some way or another, become exes.

Then there's the nuclear breakup. The one that rocks your soul. The one you prayed to God would never happen, but did. It's the one where hearts are definitely broken, seemingly beyond repair, dreams and plans come crashing down, and lives are altered forever. I had one of those. In fact, my hardest, most painful breakup was the catalyst for this book. He was a man who was in my life on and off for almost seven years, a relationship that evolved into a horribly dysfunctional love triangle.

To protect his privacy, I will call my ex-boyfriend Mr. My Big and his "other woman" I will call Natasha. If he wasn't with me, he was with Natasha. If he wasn't with Natasha, he was with me. This was what the scenario felt like throughout those seven years. Only after being *out* of such an insane situation would I be able to see the bigger picture of how I was caught in a toxic web. I was the ex-girlfriend you just didn't want your boyfriend to still have around. And what made this breakup different from all the other breakups in my life was being fully aware of Natasha, trying my best to always make things right, but in the end failing miserably.

Here is a journal entry that shows how I felt immediately after our big breakup in 2010:

Can't say time has helped any. I am hollow, distraught, in pain, lost, numb, directionless, lonely, just pure devastation . . . I cry all the time. All the time. I'd rather be under a blanket on my couch than out with people. I don't even know if talking about it helps. I miss him. I'm dying.

I met Mr. My Big at our mutual friend Ren's birthday party in early 2005. I was 29. We saw each other from across the bar and spent the rest of that evening attached at the hip. I went home that night glowing. He texted immediately, and from that moment on we dated. Dinner by the beach where he lived, cuddling on his couch listening to the waves crash, him coming to see me in the San Fernando Valley where I lived. I fell for him immediately. We had undeniable sexual chemistry, we both worked in the television industry, and we enjoyed the same sports and activities. From the get-go, it felt effortless and easy.

We would soon realize that we had met before, in the fall of 2004 when he came to a TV network I was working at to conduct an interview. I had noticed him through a glass wall that encased a conference room where he was doing the interview and had felt completely smitten. We wound up riding the elevator down together after his interview. Moments later, I called Ren, who worked with him. He filled me in and shortly after warned me to stay away. Ren said he had just moved to Los Angeles for that job and that he just broke up with a girl, Natasha, who was back in another state. There was the first red flag—his recent breakup—and I hadn't even officially met him yet. I tried to ignore this fact about his past, but it never really went away. But *he* did.

After a few months of dating, he disappeared. Suddenly. He just stopped calling and texting. Enter Ren again, who informed me Mr. My Big and Natasha had gotten back together and she was moving here. I was so pissed off and felt like a fool, but I soon let it go and started dating other people.

I ran into Mr. My Big and Natasha at a Super Bowl party in 2006. I'd later find out that Natasha said to Mr. My Big, "The minute I saw her, I knew she was trouble," about that chance encounter. She was right. I was trouble. *We* were trouble. We had a thing. An electric, magnetic thing. He texted me later that night, saying something about how it was great to see me and he loved my boots. I was seeing someone at the time. I ignored his text. Unfortunately, I'd never be that strong again.

Three months after that Super Bowl party, Mr. My Big and I wound up at Ren's for a house party and our connection picked up again. I couldn't stop the feelings, even though I knew he was with Natasha. The months after that are now a blur of sex, secret meetings, and excitement. I knew he was cheating, and I knew that I was The Other Woman, but

I didn't care. I was too caught up in the selfishness of my fantasy, the allure that he was The One. He would tell me he was breaking up with her all the time, to be patient, that things would work out. At the time, I lived about thirty minutes from him in the Valley, and I really wanted to move. Mr. My Big lived at the beach. I loved the beach, so I decided to move to the beach in the summer of 2006.

Toward the end of the summer, I was measuring a living room in an apartment I was considering when I got a text from Mr. My Big saying he had to tell me something, it probably wasn't anything I wanted to hear, and if I didn't want to talk he'd understand. I told him whatever he needed to tell me, he could say to my face. He met me at my old apartment in the Valley and proceeded to tell me he decided to not only *not* break up with Natasha, but to move in with her, because, as he put it, "I need to hit rock bottom with her to know it's not going to work." I was devastated that this seemingly perfect guy for me was once again leaving me—even though in reality I was a passenger on a rollercoaster being operated by one confused soul.

About one week after he dumped me, Mr. My Big texted me to say he thought he made a mistake. I asked where he was. At a bar with a friend, he said. Natasha was out of town for the weekend. So I drove down to the beach and wound up not leaving until the next day. He was actually living between apartments, his old one and the new one he was moving into with her. In hindsight, moving in together is the *furthest thing* from breaking up. I find it entirely embarrassing that I still went forward with relocating to the beach, where I did begin to date other people. They moved in together, and Mr. My Big and I stayed in contact as friends. But during the first few months of me living at the beach, Natasha found out about the sneaking around Mr. My Big and I had done. Upon being confronted, he lied to her about it, and then asked me to lie for him because she wanted to talk to me. She did call me with him on the phone, and I did lie for him, telling her we were only friends who met through work. I felt like crap for doing that and told him if he didn't tell her the truth I would. He told me he would, but I found out later he never did.

I'm ashamed to admit it, but even after that craziest of crazy conference calls, Mr. My Big and I secretly remained close. We'd go running together or meet up to talk. I had this saying back then, "We survived on kisses alone." During those months we were *trying* to be just friends, we would kiss every moment we were together, which just kept our passion alive. More like kept the insanity alive. I clearly was not making wise choices at all. Into the spring of 2007, he swore he was breaking up with her; for once, he had told the truth because that summer they did break up, and we slowly picked up our relationship. I was so happy. It felt right on so many levels. Finally.

For the next two and a half years or so, our relationship looked normal from the outside—traveling, meeting the families, going to our restaurants, having our favorite wines, having special nicknames for each other, sharing a bed every night, taking in the neighbor's cat, knowing our neighbors, having brunch on Sunday mornings. We shared a domestic life. We looked like a couple and I felt like we were a couple. I was in love. I had convinced myself I felt safe in the relationship. The catch about us being together, though, was he didn't tell a lot of people in his life about us, even though most had figured it out. We never went out with any of his friends, except his sports buddies. I always assumed that happened because he didn't want it getting back to Natasha that we were officially together, and at one point he did say he didn't want her to know because he didn't want to hurt her. And yet he was still hanging out with Natasha, *as friends*, he would say. Perhaps we did our own thing because I was the one he had cheated on her with and there was shame tied to that. That reasoning I could understand but it still didn't make it any easier. There was so much deception and manipulation I didn't know what to believe. Since we didn't socialize a lot, most of our time together wound up being us alone. We were in an all-consuming, intoxicating bubble.

Just past our two-year mark, early in 2010, Mr. My Big said out loud he still had feelings for Natasha. We officially broke up that day. For real. I moved out all my stuff that had accumulated at his place throughout the years, and we were done. It was ugly and really painful. After walking around in a fog for a couple of months, I moved into a little house and began to heal. But of course, you know our pattern by now; our breakups were never cut-and-dried. Going cold turkey has never been my strongest trait. For the next few months, I still hung out with him. And he continued to hang out with her.

In the fall of 2010, another of Mr. My Big's friends felt the need to let me know *he and Natasha* got back together again. About a half hour later, I showed up at his house to find her sitting on the kitchen counter while he made dinner in the sweats I had gotten him the previous year for Valentine's Day. He walked outside, closed the door behind him, and said, "It's not what you think. We're just trying to figure things out." Natasha then came out. She invited me in, and the three of us proceeded to powwow for over four hours. She and I swapped sob stories about Mr. My Big. By hour three, we were all drinking hard liquor. I swear, Mr. My Big needed a diaper. In the end, it was me that left the home I had shared so many nights with him, with her still in it. A lot of tears.

After that night, I couldn't conceive of staying at the beach just blocks away from them, so the next day I was on a plane to join my friend Andrea in Atlanta on a business trip. I stayed in the hotel bed most of the time. At one point, Andrea pulled back the curtains to let the light in and screamed, "If you don't get out of bed now I'm going to post a picture of you on Facebook looking like you do right now with the caption, 'He chose the other one.'" That set me straight. I slowly got on with my life.

A few months later, I bumped into Mr. My Big running on the bike path near the beach. My stomach dropped when I saw him. I'm not going to lie, I was really glad to see him. We caught up over a long walk. He said he wasn't completely happy with Natasha, they weren't living together yet, and he wasn't sure he did the right thing getting back together with her. He also said, "I love you"—something he could *never* say during our relationship.

At the time, I was wearing the iPod he had gotten me for the holidays a few years earlier. With the gift, he also gave me his entire library of music. So at that impromptu meeting on the bike path, I said, "You know, I'm still listening to the same music you gave me, because this iPod is connected to your iTunes. I can't add music to it." He replied, "Well, you could either erase all the music I gave you, or I can take it from you now and give you new music."

I gave him the iPod. I accepted his invitation to put me back in his life. I said yes to seeing him again, yes to getting sucked back into his web of deceit and control and lies. The next day, I got an IM from him about what type of music I wanted on the iPod. The rest, sadly, is history. Here it was, early 2011, a year after our big breakup, and we were back in each other's lives. We would see each other all the time, have sleepovers when we could, and have hours and hours of conversations. Tucked neatly into one of our talks was Mr. My Big telling me he bought an engagement ring for Natasha, but wasn't sure she was The One. He told me all of his reservations about their relationship but this is my book, not his, and so I will leave his details out. Just know, I heard everything he was saying and honestly could not see the two of them romantically together.

Even knowing he bought a ring for her, just hearing him say he wasn't sure he wanted to give it to her was enough for me to try to save us. I actually believed him when he told me, "As long as she doesn't find out about us, we can be together." I couldn't for the life of me understand why he didn't just leave her. Let me tell you, being seemingly strung along by a guy you are in love with is brutal. I don't know if Natasha ever figured out Mr. My Big and I were hanging out again, but I believe every woman knows when her man is elsewhere, physically or mentally. If your man is cheating on you, you know.

In the fall of 2011, Mr. My Big and I were inside my house. We were upstairs in my bedroom. We were on the floor. I was sitting in his lap, my legs and arms wrapped tight around him. His arms and legs were wrapped around me. I was crying. Nothing was changing with any of it. I knew I wanted and deserved more. I had to walk away. We decided to not see or talk to each other for a while. See how it went. How it went was, she saw a Facebook post on my wall from one of my friends with his name on it, he proposed to Natasha a few weeks later and wasn't the one to tell me he did it.

It was October, my birthday month. I turned 36. A few weeks after he had been to my house, I saw him driving by my place when I was pulling onto my street. Mr. My Big pulled over and we talked outside my house for a few minutes. I don't recall the conversation, but I remember the vibe was sad. Yet within the *next few days*, Mr. My Big gave Natasha the ring and he did not tell me he was going to do it. I wouldn't come to figure all this timing out until Ren called to tell me two weeks later. Ren said he wanted to wait until after my birthday passed. Ren had watched Mr. My Big and I from the beginning and has apologized on numerous occasions for introducing us.

Six months after they got engaged, they got married.

Yep, that girl in the other state I learned about in the fall of 2004 would wind up being the girl he ultimately married in 2012. I'd be the girl he kept going back to for almost seven years while he figured it out, and that mutual friend who I called inquiring about him in the first place would be the one to tell me, almost seven years after that first encounter, they were engaged.

The next few months were beyond surreal. Even when the dust settled after their engagement, I was still a mess. It was over. I had no more fight left, and navigating through the heartbreak was tough. I didn't pick up the phone if anyone called. I left text messages unanswered. I went to my hometown of New York City for a couple of weeks to lose myself in the energy of the streets. That always makes me feel better. One of the toughest things to swallow during that time was the fact that I truly believed he followed through with the engagement and marriage because that's what he thought was the proper thing to do, and there wasn't a damn thing I could do about it. I couldn't for the life of me comprehend why she stayed with him either, but then again, I had my own feelings to sort through. I had to finally let it go and let me tell you, I didn't want to.

My emotions were all over the place—depression, anger, rage, resentment, love, passion, and loneliness. I wanted to maybe forgive because that's what "they" said I needed to do to move on, but I hadn't a clue how to do it. I had come so far in love, and yet I was standing there without him. I'd say ultimately losing Mr. My Big was like going through withdrawal from heroin. I've never done heroin, but I can imagine that's what it's like. It took days for that initial sick, empty feeling to pass, but it did. Moping throughout the following weeks became the norm. A few months went by before I was able to feel somewhat like myself again.

To quote one of my favorite TV shows of all time, *Sex and the City*, Carrie says after her breakup with Berger, "The loneliness is palpable." It's true. It's lonely, it's hard, and you just may want to die. But you're not going to. You'll hate life for a long time. But your life is about to change. The way you view yourself and the world is about to change. And change is good. The key is not to spend too much time feeling sorry for yourself. A pity party that goes on too long won't help you.

I am not proud of my behavior. After some professional help on the matter, I figured out that what we shared was codependency more than love. I constantly put his needs before my own and, in doing so, I neglected to fully take care of myself. The old me needed to be in that spot. The new me couldn't even imagine it. If you gave away your power in your relationship, you certainly shouldn't continue giving it to him after the two of you have broken up. Ease out of the cycle. Easier said than done, I know.

Many women have that guy they go back to. Heartbreak after heartbreak. Even if her man tells her straight up he doesn't want to get back together. Women tell the guys they're strong enough to handle the breakup sex, they won't get attached, they understand the scenario, and that it's all good. It's all *lies*. Most women I know are not strong enough to do any of that, but for some reason they lie to themselves and to the guy that they can do it. If you choose to go back to a guy who has repeatedly hurt you, you have no one to blame for the repercussions but yourself. You are signing up for that misery.

There is something to be said for staying in a relationship for as long as you can, fighting for a person you care deeply about. But love shouldn't be so hard, and when it is, you're chasing something that isn't meant to be in your life. So, what do you do? Sometimes, you just hold on for dear life to someone who ultimately is going to exit your life and it's going to bring pain.

Were you completely blindsided by *your* breakup? Can you really sit there and say you didn't have a clue you guys were doomed? That's usually the toughest thing to admit to yourself, that you really *did* see it coming. As for the reason you and your man broke up—whatever it is—let it go. Get off the story of what happened as soon as possible, because in the end it's never about the story. It's about the patterns, behaviors, and choices you made that put you in that scenario. That's where the work lies. All you need to know is you loved, you may have not been loved in return, you stayed a really long time trying to make it work, and now here you are. Figure out how you got to the place you are right now. That's when you'll begin to see the bigger picture.

No one wants to experience the agony of heartbreak. It disrupts your status quo and forces you to go completely out of your comfort zone. Millions of women before you have undergone the painful experience of heartbreak, have struggled to get back on their feet only to reclaim their lives and emerge on the other side wiser and stronger. Breakups are always going to be challenging and uncomfortable, but they're a must in the world of dating when you're in search of your soul mate.

In the pages that follow is my post-breakup road map to finding yourself again, a stronger, wiser self. I shape the lessons I learned into frank and practical advice, providing you with simple and effective ways to move on with your life. With time and the right approach, your heart will heal and you will be ready to face the world with newfound strength and wisdom. Each chapter is a different piece of advice someone gave me on how to get through the breakup. I talk about if it worked or didn't work for me, and why. I detail going through the highs and lows from the early days of the initial split to how I moved on. No one said it was going to be easy, but you will learn you are definitely not alone, and it will make the road a little less bumpy.

While sometimes exhilarating, the pursuit of finding a life partner also can be exhausting. Many lovers and boyfriends come along to pass the time until we find The One. These people make our lives rich with promise, security, and safety in a world that oftentimes seems to hold none beyond our very own front door. It can be scary out there and, no doubt, having a partner in crime with whom to tackle it makes the journey that much easier. So what happens when that partner of yours walks out of the very front door that once kept the two of you in your own little bubble? What happens when the bubble bursts? Of course, you already know how it ends. This book is about what happens after it ends.

 YOUR TURN: Acknowledge the breakup. Start reading.

DON'T BE ALONE

He left you. Or you left him. Either way, you feel completely alone in this world. All of a sudden, your man is not next to you, and the pain is almost unbearable. Those first minutes, hours, days, and weeks into the breakup are horrendous. You almost have an out-of-body experience thing going on. Your eyeballs hurt from crying and your lack of sleep. It's like you're walking around in a fog. You want to die, you think you might die, but you don't. You're still breathing. That gut-wrenching feeling doesn't kill you. How is that possible that you are actually alive while feeling this awful?

So what do you do? Where do you go? Do you just go back to your old apartment and pretend the relationship never existed? Do you go out with friends tonight? Should you be alone and fend for yourself? The answers to these questions are no, you can't pretend it never happened; yes, go out with your friends; and no, do not be alone. During the first few days after your breakup, I will stress that you should not be alone.

The reasons are quite obvious. You are so beyond lost after a breakup, and it's paralyzing. With your mind in such a dark place you need help from loved ones. You are used to having someone there. Your man is not there anymore, so go find people.

While in the relationship with Mr. My Big, I used to say that going to bed and waking up with him were the best parts of my day. There are no better moments than waking up in a slightly sweaty bed next to the man you love and crawling into an already broken-in bed at the end of the day with the person you love. Post-breakup, mornings became the worst part of my day. Nighttime was rough, too. I found myself not wanting to turn off the TV at the end of the night, because that meant the house went quiet. After about a month, I got used to the loneliness and the quiet, which in turn made it really hard to re-engage with people. It will become quite easy to fall into a life of depression and solitude if you allow it. If you stay in that sphere of solitude for too long, it will become beyond difficult to get yourself out of it. Don't go there. *Choose* not to go there. You have to choose it for yourself. Start now.

You may find yourself terrified of being alone, which becomes confusing because what this time *does not* refer to is having another man in your bed. Using a guy to fill the void in your life will only make the void feel worse later. There is a big difference between rebounding with another guy to temper the pain and staying close to good friends and family. I recently had dinner with my friend Angelina, who is always in and out of relationships. At the start of each one, she confesses that the guy of the moment is The One and that she's marrying him. Needless to say, our latest dinner was about her latest breakup. She was about four weeks into it and seemed to be doing okay under the circumstances. She finally confessed that she was starting to see the pattern she was falling into with men. She told me she is afraid to be alone, and so goes from boyfriend to boyfriend so she doesn't have to feel the sharp pain of solitude. I reminded her, as I remind all of you, that sharp pain is necessary to feel at this point. It *does* go away.

Surround yourself with people you love and who love you back. You need to be nurtured and taken care of at this point. I thought Mr. My Big was my base. My best friend. I felt I could do anything, accomplish any goal, achieve any dream, just knowing he had my back (or so I thought). But once that base goes away, it almost feels as though you have nothing to stand on anymore, nothing holding you up when you fall. Like there isn't a foundation to put your two feet on anymore. Post-breakup is the crucial time to get yourself a new base or foundation as quickly as possible. A base helps support whatever stands on it. In order for change to occur, you need a good foundation from which to start. And again, I do not mean another man.

My base is and always has been family. Just after a breakup, you will rely on your family a lot. My mom, dad, and sister have always been my support system. I needed them more than ever after my breakup, but I was on the West Coast and they were all on the East Coast. With mom and dad retired in Florida and my sister, brother-in-law, and nephew in New York, I flew across the country for long weekends about once a month to be with them, and I still do. During that time, you could either find me wandering the streets of New York City or sunbathing by the pool. It was my time near my family, and that's all that mattered. Go where the support is. Granted, I cried on the plane and moped around my family's places when I got there, but the point is I was with people who loved me and cared for me. It became my saving grace. I understand that flying across the country may not seem smart considering you have to buy plane tickets, but to be honest, you won't miss the money. You've been saving for a rainy day; well, guess what, it's raining. It's raining with thunder and lightning and dark clouds looming for days. The storm is here to stay. Buy the tickets.

Your family is going to be the one group who will not care that all of a sudden you're needing them 24/7. They probably won't say things like, "Oh, now you want to come and hang out with us?" or "Why weren't you there when I needed you?" I was so busted up during that time, the last thing I needed was a guilt trip about why I wanted to hang out with my family more than usual. I just wanted to be taken in, and that's exactly what they did for me. Even before the breakup, I always called my mom and dad. Talking to the parents makes any crappy situation that much more bearable. My dad is a retired high school guidance counselor, and I got very used to calling him up and saying, "Okay, Dad, I need your guidance counselor hat on." And he'd say, "Okay, go." Unconditional support. Go find it.

My nephew was born a few months after my breakup, and it was almost like a delivery from God. I wrote the dedication to this book before I actually wrote the book. My munchkin came into my life at just the exact moment I needed to be injected with unconditional love, joy, and warmth. My nephew soaked up all the love I needed to share, and he was so willing to take it. He actually wants to talk to me, hug, kiss, and play with me all the time. Especially after that breakup, that's *exactly* what I needed.

I asked my sister to describe for me what I was like in those dark moments when I'd come to visit. She replied in an email with the subject line, "Five Words of the Past You." The email read:

*I always blanked on what to write other than some words—
unreasonable, defensive, stubborn, blinded, obsessed. By definition,
they each speak volumes. Adding "very" in front of each would
sum up some of the more colorful times. Funny how I used the
word "colorful," since you would always wear black, especially nail
polish, as you weren't feeling any color. It says a lot that you can
now read this and chuckle, because the you of a few years ago*

wouldn't have been able to do that. Hence, they are five words of
the past you. :) XO.

Being far away from your family for everyday life is a bit tricky,
but life is still totally doable. Just make sure you are always with your
friends. Accept all invitations. Sleep at their houses, meet them wherever
they are going, and never say no when they ask to come over. Bring your
laundry over to do at a friend's house, bring food and wine, or watch TV
with them. Let your friends cook you dinner. Go to their couches to cry.
It gets you out of the house and with people who love you.

Two of my dear friends, a married couple who witnessed from
start to finish the insanity of my relationship, have two children. The
running joke is that I am the third child. During the first weekend
after the breakup, this family set me up in their daughter's room and
let me sleep there. That is what it came down to: a young girl giving
up her pink, princess-themed bedroom for me. That's unconditional
love and friendship. The days and nights in their home dedicated to
drinking wine and crying about my relationship were necessary. This
family lives only a few blocks away from me, and I couldn't have
gotten through that time without them. To this day, I always know
I have a place to retire at the end of the day for dinner, wine, good
company, or a warm bed if need be. Here's what my friend/the mom
said of that time:

Lesley is known in our house as Our Teenage Daughter or Crazy
Lesley. Terms of endearment, for sure. She was nuts during those
years. My then 8- and 9-year-old kids were giving her relationship
advice. I was making the couch into a bed for her, or she would sleep
in the pinkalicious 8-year-old's room. Really. She had lost her mind.
However, as it is with losing one's mind, the sturdy and resourceful
always seem to find it. At some point. We knew she would.

This is the same friend who, during the bad days after my breakup, looked at me over burgers, fries, and wine and said, "This is your book!" Thanks, friend.

I do have some of the greatest girlfriends on the planet. The group is made up of businesswomen, actresses, housewives, artists—you name it, we have it in our bunch. They each bring something unique to the table, and that's what makes the group so great. I noticed something about this group of women, though. No matter how successful the friend is, no matter what is going on in their career—be it landing a massive movie role, getting that promotion, or finally getting more money for their start-up—there is always room in our conversations to talk about men and our love lives. I'm sure your girlfriends are the same way, which only further emphasizes my point that when you're going through a breakup, these are the people you're going to want to be around to discuss it.

You want to surround yourself with people who know what you're going through *and* who have been in your shoes. They'll know when to talk, when to listen, and when to just let you be. It's especially sweet considering my friends were the same group who watched me repeatedly, for years, get my heart broken by Mr. My Big, and the same friends who listened to me talk about the heartbreak I was experiencing over and over again. If these people are your best friends, they won't think twice about taking care of you for a while.

When your friends aren't around, getting up and going to work will become your next saving grace, because your coworkers will be there to support you, too. Their mere presence around you will make you feel less alone. For me, there's one writer I'm close with at work I would always chat with about my love life. He has a Buddha tattoo on his arm. He's married with two kids, and gets it. He always listened and had great things to say. When I recently spoke to him about this book, he recalled what I was like during the breakup. He said I got mad a lot and would always snap at him for no reason. He also said that no matter what he said to me, I would always start to cry. We're still friends, and he never turned his back on me.

So we've got your family, your friends, and your coworkers. I'd say that's an awesome collection of folks to be spending time with right now. And besides the random hookups I've already said will not make you feel better and will no doubt make you feel worse than you already do (more on that later), there *are* other people I would advise you *not* to hang out with. These people consist of *his* friends, or even the group of *mutual friends* you and your ex-boyfriend once shared. You need to create your own world, not stay in his. The mutual friends thing just won't work anymore, because all you'll want to do is ask them questions about your ex, which, for starters, will make you look desperate and reaching. More importantly, you will never be able to move on from this guy while having a constant reminder of him in your face. I tried staying friends with Mr. My Big's posse for a bit, but it didn't work. All we would wind up doing, in some roundabout way, was talking about Mr. My Big, and that's no fun. It's not worth it.

For some, the best kind of companionship is the four-legged kind. Nothing says unconditional love like a furry little cat or dog. They are always there, they will always love you, and they will never break your heart. The only reason I never got a cat or a dog is because I travel so much and I didn't want to do that to any little guy. I had two parakeets, Fred and Ginger, that I had rescued when I first moved to LA. Ginger lived for fourteen years, outliving two of her bird boyfriends, Fred and another boy bird I named Wasabi. Tough chick, that Ginger. She passed away a few years after my breakup, but I know she waited until just that time to make sure I was okay on my own. Animals are nutty like that. They know. But if you're starting fresh and don't have the burden of a lot of travel, consider some adorable animal you can cuddle with on the couch. Sometimes having a ridiculously cute, furry pet can prevent a spiral into absolute insanity, and that is exactly what you should be looking for following a breakup. Stopping the insanity.

Also, in this time of crisis, misery is not good company. Rather, this is when you need to rid yourself of all the negative people in your life, all those folks who never have anything positive to say and are always bitching and moaning about something. One positive, uplifting friend who brings out the best in you, especially after a breakup, is far better than ten acquaintances who have nothing else to do than complain and keep you down. You've already been down enough.

 YOUR TURN: Whom do you trust? Whom could you be with at your worst and know they would never judge you? Write down their names, and go to those people.

LET THE TEARS FLOW

My spiritual psychology graduate school professor (more on my studies later) said in class once, "The amount you grieve is equal to the amount you loved." I was so glad he said that, because after all the breakups with Mr. My Big put together, it was almost like I needed his permission to be so sad. There were days when life literally seemed just too much to handle. Love can make us do crazy things, grand things, insane things, passionate things, and life-altering things. And love can make us cry. After months of crying in my car, in my shower, at birthday parties, at work, going to sleep, waking up in the morning, in yoga class, even during dance class, I was beginning to wonder why it was taking me so long to feel better. Until I found out it was really okay to cry for as long as I needed to, I thought all that blubbering was a bad thing.

Don't be afraid to express your emotions. Get 'em out. Not only is crying not wrong, it's probably the healthiest thing you can do. It means you really loved someone and you are grieving that loss. Of course tears are going to fall. Sobbing helps relieve all that tension you're holding onto for dear life. Holding on for dear life is maybe what got you into this state in the first place.

You are a human being, not a robot. It's human to become attached to another human. Needless to say, after a breakup you have to detach from that other person. This attaching and detaching cycle can be really painful, and with pain usually comes tears. It is the most natural thing in the world to have to recover from an event this traumatic. For many months, the pain will feel like a punch that won't stop aching. I found when I tried to push down the pain and not cry, it didn't work; all it did was bottle it up and store it for later. If you don't mourn the breakup now, you're just going to keep all those feelings inside, and those feelings will for sure manifest themselves in other ways—stomach problems, bad skin, achy joints, headaches, you name it. Your body will feel it and will show it.

Cry until you are exhausted. You usually will feel better after a good cry. There is a reason for that. You are releasing the pain one tear at a time. When someone tells you to stop crying about him already, don't listen. Crying is a natural part of healing. If you *didn't* cry, I'd think there was something wrong with you. Grief is a process, two steps forward, one step back. It's the way we get through the shifts in our lives, because if you don't hit bottom, you can never rise up stronger and wiser. Funny thing about grief though, it doesn't kill you. When in the throes of that pain, our survival instincts kick in and take over, and that is what keeps us going. You're devastated but you are not destroyed. Remember that.

While in the thick of all those tears and sadness though, there's no proper way to navigate through the pain. You can't MapQuest it and get from point A to point B smoothly. With all the questions you may ask friends and family about how to feel better, nobody can really give you the right answer. Even if they try, it's never going to be anything you want to hear. Not at this stage anyway. Your man isn't there anymore and he's not coming back, that's all you need to know.

I'm sure you've heard of the stages of grief everyone goes through and talks about. One day you're feeling one way, the next, another. I'm feeling really lethargic today; will I feel rage tomorrow? I woke up really angry this morning; will I feel forgiveness by sunset? Someone came up with these stages of grief. The name for it is the Kübler-Ross model, from Elizabeth Kübler-Ross's book *On Death and Dying*. Kübler-Ross was a Swiss American psychiatrist and a pioneer on the subject of death. The five stages of the Kübler-Ross model are denial, anger, bargaining, depression, and acceptance. You will no doubt find yourself going back and forth through all the stages for months.

For me, the denial stage, or the "shock stage" as I like to call it, happened for at least the first few months. I'd wake up in the morning and for a split second all was well in the world. Then I'd be reminded of my loss. You might not believe it all actually happened. The anger stage I remember really well. It's almost like you don't know what to do with it. You'll be angry about everything. The bargaining one was a real doozy. I felt like I was bargaining for almost a year and a half. Half the time with him. Just plain exhausting. After denial, anger, and bargaining you move into depression. If you've never felt sadness from a loss, this stage will hit you pretty hard. In this stage, questions like "Why now?" and "Why me?" can pop up into your head. As you will come to see and learn, the answers aren't out there, they are inside you.

When you enter the acceptance stage, all you have to do is surrender. The good news is this stage usually happens naturally, because you won't have anything left in you to try and make it happen. Forcing something to happen won't work anyway. Surrender is a powerful thing. To surrender is to let it go. Give over to a higher power, whatever that means to you. Let go of the reins for a minute, let the universe catch up with you, and just stop pushing. There will come a time when you put your hands up and say, "I'm not going to know all the answers," and move on from a calmer place, not the chaos.

Kübler-Ross's groundbreaking book is about the experience of people close to death and those caring for them. Even so, breakups are sort of like a death. You are mourning a loss. Experiencing loss, however it's presented in your life, will affect you the same way. The blessing in this natural process is that after death comes rebirth.

If you feel there is something deeper going on besides just the normal sadness from a breakup, we tackle that later in the book. Just know *wherever* you find yourself, it's okay. One thing I can almost guarantee is that after you've gone through boxes of tissues, one day you will find yourself laughing. Laughter and a sense of humor will be key ingredients to surviving your broken heart. Like my sister said, one day you are going to laugh at your story and all the silly things you did during that relationship. I sure have, and you will too. Eventually, this pain of yours, this hurt and sadness, will lead to service. You will be able to help other women going through the same emotions.

People are going to ask you all the time, "How are you?" and "How are you feeling?" There's really no good answer, so I think it's best to start with the truth. Say, "I'm heartbroken, but okay." The okay part means you are surviving and someday soon you will be back in the game.

 YOUR TURN: Cry.

STEP AWAY FROM THE COMPUTER

The more a man pushes a woman away, the more it seems many women, including my former self, try to pull themselves closer by any means possible. He's walking away. Let him go. Unfortunately, it being the twenty-first century, this man can always be right at your fingertips if you let him. While Facebook, Twitter, Instagram, and all the other marvelous ways we stay connected are great, these technological advances were not invented so you could stalk your ex-boyfriend or the girl he is currently dating. You are torturing yourself.

Picture my mother standing in front of you, waving her hands dramatically and yelling, "Step awaaaay from the computer!" I know most of you don't know my mother. Just picture a very smart woman trying to kick some sense into you at one of your low moments. She always says this to me when I get a tad obsessed about anything. It's her way of saying, step away from the situation.

Nowadays, breakups are tricky because it's not like one day you decide it's over and then you never see, talk to, or hear of that person again. Your ex can stay around in your life for as long as you allow him to—physically, emotionally, spiritually, mentally, and, most importantly these days, *technologically*. If, after your breakup, you remain friends with him on Facebook or you still follow him on Twitter, be prepared for your life to be more miserable than it needs to be right now. Need I remind you that you have the control, right in those little hands of yours, to keep your ex as far away as possible. It's for your own well-being. Choose wisely here, because if you don't, you are only hurting yourself. The longer you keep this guy's presence around, in person, in your contact list, and especially in social media, the longer it will take you to move on with your life. The right thing to do always seems to be hardest thing to do, but you can do this. Unfriend. Unfollow. Delete.

Technology has made it borderline impossible to let someone go. Sometimes I think the Internet is a cruel, nasty joke. The web was not at all meant for anyone trying to get over someone. It is a dark, endless place that never forgets. Breakups definitely aren't what they used to be. At the time of mine, the iPhone was only around for a year or so. Facebook was very popular, but I didn't use Twitter yet, and I didn't even know what Instagram was. It will take every morsel of strength and bit of willpower you have not to stalk your ex's social media accounts, whether you unfriend and unfollow him or not. It's a sad but true fact of our modern times that even after your relationship is over, if your man is active on social media, you will be able to find out exactly what he is doing at any given moment. Who he's hanging out with, where he's been, and where he's going. Sadly, it'll probably look like he's having a damn good time, while you are curled up in a blanket being sad.

When it comes down to it, all you are really trying to do with this ex-boyfriend cyber-stalking thing is maintain some sort of connection to him. I get it, you want to be close to him, but this is not the way to do it, and it's not healthy. I'm all for modern technology and the gobs of advancements we've made in the field, but when it comes to a broken heart, I almost wish we were back in the age before computers because it would be so much easier to move on from a person!

Let's address how to deal with the big four:

1) Google. Please ladies, stop Googling your ex-boyfriend's name. Just stop. All it's going to get you, really, is you possibly learning something about him that will probably hurt you more anyway. Whoever first coined the phrase, "Ignorance is bliss," was right. Whatever you see will haunt you. Do you want to know when his wedding date is? Or where he's registered? Yeah, I don't think so. So don't Google their names. Especially don't Google his name with his new girlfriend or fiancée's name.

2) Twitter. Stop stalking his Twitter feed. How about you unfollow him for a while? See how that feels. You don't need to see where he's been, with whom he's hanging out, whose tweets he's favoriting, and who's mentioning his name. You are not going to win that war, nor will you ever move on. So you see what party he's at or whom he's hanging out with, big deal. What is that going to do for you, really? You weren't there, nor are you going to be invited to the next party. You hovering over his feed won't bring you anything but pain and suffering. No joy will come from that task. And all this Twitter behavioral advice goes for his Instagram account as well.

3) Instagram. Stop following him and stop scrolling through your ex-boyfriend's feed. Stop giving him heart-shaped "likes" next to all his photos hoping he will be reminded of you. Liking an image, or even worse leaving a comment on one of them, will have the reverse effect you're going for. Just a guess here; he probably loves the attention, but

that does not mean he wants to get back together with you. Put up your own photos of yourself doing something fun. Let *him* wonder where you are and what *you're* doing. This isn't *technically* about revenge, but the best way to portray to your ex how you're doing without him is to show him that your life is better without him in it. Even if you're not there yet. You will be.

4) Facebook. This social media site could emotionally damage you and it will prevent you from ever healing, growing, and moving on gracefully if you don't chill out on the obsessive watching of his page. Seriously, Mark Zuckerberg made it so hard post-breakup. Ladies, stop going to your ex-boyfriend's Facebook page and scrolling through his wall for updates and staring at his new pictures. Stop clicking on all the names of new people with whom he's become friends. All this will do is lead to more heartache and more pain. Are you ready, *really* ready, to discover he has another girlfriend? I don't think you are. Do you want to see how happy he looks now that he doesn't have you in his life? Probably not. Constantly hovering over his Facebook wall is pure madness and it won't help you move on. You're wasting a lot of time and causing yourself more grief. Try unfriending him and see how it feels. You may just feel lighter.

The same rule applies to his friends' Facebook pages, too. Stop the insanity. If you don't stop now, it will only be harder to stop later. Oh, and don't bash your ex on Facebook, or any other social media site for that matter. You'll regret it. You're an adult, act like one. I should have cut and run when Mr. My Big refused to title himself as being "in a relationship" on Facebook. As juvenile as that sounds, at the time, it meant a lot. I should have further gotten a clue when he canceled his Facebook account.

Regardless of whether you're stalking his feeds or not, get your head out of your phone and live a little. There are infinite experiences to be had and new people (men!) to meet right in front of you. If you keep your face buried in that computer screen in your hand, you will miss it all. Even though your ex looks super cute on Instagram, there is no way he is going to reach out and touch you. I know, in that other Instagram photo it looks like he's dating the entire group of girls he's posing with, but obsessing about it will get you nowhere. Furthermore, making up a story in your head about what you see on his feed or in his pictures will drive you crazy. The picture was taken and you weren't there. So go live your own life and stop living vicariously through his new life and his friends' lives. You can't join his party. No app in the world is going to bring you two back together, nor will an app bring you closer to human contact than actual human contact will. Lift up your head, stop spying on your ex, and rejoin the world, because with human contact, spirits will be lifted and hearts will be healed.

Here's another thing. If you're in a gray area of the relationship where you've already broken up but you're still sleeping with them occasionally and still totally in love with them and you then snoop, be prepared. Because if you do, you're going to find out things you may not like. And that's going to suck even more than if you were just snooping and weren't seeing them anymore. If you're still hanging out with them, that means you're still holding onto some semblance of hope you two would get back together. So, here's what's going to happen. You're going to snoop and find out they're still hanging out with their other ex, or better yet they're marrying their ex, or you're going to find out whom the new girlfriend is. Social media doesn't sugarcoat anything and it does not lie to make you feel better. You have now seen with your own eyes that there is someone else in his life and that person isn't you. No amount of willing, stalking, or pining will make you that girl. But even when the truth is staring you in the face, you will attempt to justify to yourself and to everyone around you that there's still a very good reason you're holding on. What's the reason, again?

So you've snooped and now you have very valuable information at your disposal. What are you going to do? Don't do anything about it, and you're lying to yourself, and you're f'ed. Great, you've wasted more time. Do nothing and you are to blame for whatever happens next. Do something about it and you're f'ed anyway, but at least you got out early enough and you can move onto the healing part instead of being strung along for six more months. Do something and you take back your life. Snoop, and you really do hold the power because you will know the truth. You already hold the power regardless, but now this is the universe showing you what's up. Mess with the universe and it will mess with you back. Standing up for yourself sometimes can be the hardest thing you'll ever do, but you will be standing up for your life.

If you want to continue cyber-stalking your ex, go ahead. I can't physically stop you, but be sure to let me know how that part of the moving-on process works out for you. It won't work out for you, but let me know if it does. You may know something I don't. Also, if you do keep up the improper digging, you could be looking at a restraining order. And that definitely won't end pretty. Go out, get a life, and stop obsessing about his.

 YOUR TURN: Unfriend your ex-boyfriend on Facebook. Stop following him on Twitter and Instagram. Not later, when you finish this book. Now!

SCULPT YOUR POST-BREAKUP BODY

Often, in film and television when some girl is going through a breakup, the script has the depressed girl eating an entire tub of Ben & Jerry's ice cream. I honestly don't know any woman who really does that or where the idea came from, but the girl is always sitting there with that small frozen container in her hand and a big spoon in the other. She's puffy and sad and devouring her ice cream. Really? I have never sat in one place for a long period of time downing the Chunky Monkey. But the whole eating/not eating, losing weight/gaining weight issue after a breakup *is* definitely relatable.

Usually right after the initial sting of the breakup, you're not going to be very hungry. You won't have an appetite and may drop a few pounds. I call it the breakup body. That look is not something you want to achieve, because it means you didn't get that figure the proper way but got it because you weren't eating. How skinny I had become, the bones protruding from my chest after my split, was the first thing my mother noticed about me. When my mom comments about how little I am I usually just shrug it off, but at that moment in my life, I knew she was right. It was never a conscious choice not to put food in my mouth. I just had an aching knot in my gut for so long the last thing I could conceive of was eating a whole lot. Being *thirsty* was another story. (We tackle alcohol later in the book.)

After a breakup, you're going to lose your appetite and you're going to lose weight. Eventually though, that dull feeling you have in your stomach will go away and you *will* find yourself wanting to eat again. No doubt your friends and family will want to put food in your belly. They are going to cook for you and you should let them. And comfort food is called *comfort* food for a reason. Someone, somewhere gave it that label because comfort food makes us feel great in a time of need. If it's not ice cream, maybe it's takeout Chinese, pizza, mac and cheese, potato chips, or guacamole and tortillas. You name it, if it feels good going down, you should start eating it, within reason, after a breakup.

You may even start cooking meals for yourself, although I found after my breakup the last thing I wanted to do was cook for one. It just made me feel lonelier. But if you're the type of woman who likes to try out a new recipe and you like cooking for yourself, go for it. What a great way to spend your time post-split. As you start to get your appetite back, you will gain some of your weight back. There will come a time months after your breakup when you'll say to yourself, "Dang, I was so skinny back then. I want that body again!" The good news is you can get something similar to that body, but now in a healthy, nutritious way.

Keep. Moving. Exercise will make you feel better. It's a fact. Do not rush into being a superwoman at the gym or joining a team to run a marathon right after the breakup. That will come with time. For starters, I suggest keeping it simple by just getting up off the couch and going for a walk. Walking gets the heart pumping and gets your mind focusing on all the nature within your reach. Just allowing your eyes to see something besides the walls of your home is a start. It's time to change up the scenery.

There's a reason I'm telling you not to go all out on the treadmill just yet. When you are weak, you tire more easily. And usually the last thing you're thinking about while going through a messy breakup is how you can get rock-solid abs or how you want to burn enough calories to fit into your skinny jeans. You're not going to *want* to go the gym. So don't. Wait until your mind is in line with your body before going back to the gym. Once your strength *is* back and you've gained a few pounds, you'll be able to release all the hate, anger, and frustration you have about the man who broke your heart on that poor piece of gym equipment. That anger is not going anywhere. But if you push yourself too hard in the beginning, you will wind up on the floor passed out. Anything related to you lying on the floor is a stage we are trying to move you away from.

When you *are* ready, go get it. Working out all the grief you're holding onto is such an amazing release for your body. You can finally start to release your emotions, pent-up anger, and toxic energy that's been pumping through your veins. When you exercise, you are reducing stress by boosting your mood and releasing things called endorphins, which are your brain's feel-good neurotransmitters. And starting to feel good is what this process is all about.

Once I got healthy again, which I would say took about a month or two, that's when I hit the gym hard. I took my spin classes till I waddled out the door, went to yoga and Pilates class to strengthen my core and my mind, and walked miles upon miles on the path by the beach near my house. I am a dancer and dance class is where I thrive. So back to the dance studio I went, and I killed it. How sweet it was. Whatever source of exercise or movement you can muster up, do it. Take your time to not eat and be pathetic. I am giving you permission to do so for a short while, but then throw on some killer music and get on with it.

About a year later, I was so inspired that I felt the need to change up my workout routine and hired a personal trainer. It's all about making your world look different than it used to. I think it's a great idea if you can afford one-on-one training. It kick-starts your mind and body into doing exercises you would never do on your own, and after a while you really start to notice a difference in your physical being. So there's the whole vanity/health thing, plus you have your own personal cheerleader leading the way.

Back to yoga. It was in the tail end of my relationship when I started to pick up this practice. I immediately fell in love with it. Yoga is powerful exercise that incorporates body, mind, and soul. When I am on that yoga mat, in that yoga room, nothing else matters. Especially when I'm stressed out or anxiety ridden, being in the yoga room with soft, angelic music playing literally melts away my tension. The tension that remains is in the muscles I'm working out, and it feels fantastic. One thing I just love about my practice is my yoga teacher. Her voice is soothing and transports me to a safe space. Especially if you're going through a breakup, taking up yoga can help you so much in centering yourself and finding some peace and balance, if just for a short while. That short while may soon turn into a longer while, and may later turn into most of the time. I started going a few times a week. Each time I got stronger and more knowledgeable on the poses. As the weeks, months, and now years go by, my body and mind crave it. Yoga is where I go to check out, to tone up, and to rebalance my life. I don't even bring my iPhone into the gym with me. I keep it in the car.

I was so excited to talk about yoga in this chapter that I took my notepad into class one day to write down some of the wonderful phrases my teacher says during class just to illustrate how transforming it is. Here goes:

Stay calm. I know it's tough sometimes. Use your breath for that.
Wobbly is okay. It's what you do after that matters.
Being wobbly is how we get stronger.
Wobbly now means strength next time.
Quiet the mind.
You are in control of your center of gravity.
Lift the heart.
Focus.
Patience and breathing.
If you can't execute a pose, use help. That's what the blocks
    are for. Support.
Slow equals strength.
Namaste.

Don't you feel better already by just reading this stuff? It really does work. But going to the gym doesn't mean only yoga class, lifting weights, spinning, or boot camp. If it's available at your health club, use the steam room or sauna in the ladies locker room and just be. Sitting there for a few minutes, breathing deeply, will be really soothing and will feel so good.

Feel like shit. Ease into feeling a bit better. Become a warrior. Working out will help you get there.

 YOUR TURN: Write down at least five positive things exercising does for you. If you aren't a member of a gym yet, I recommend joining one. Also, what type of music do you love? Fill your music player with all your favorite jams, get out of the house, and get your feet moving.

WRITE ABOUT IT

Going through a breakup is a bummer. There's no real way around that fact. You don't want to go out, you don't want to see your friends or family, you don't want to exercise, and you don't really feel like watching movies or television. After the phase where you need to be with someone at all times, and after maybe you've curbed cyber-stalking your ex, you will eventually start to crave some time to sit silently with your thoughts. Your friends and family have heard it all, and you certainly can't keep going back to your ex and asking, "Why?" There's going to come a time when you have to get the thoughts out that are in your head in some way or another. The best solution is to take pen to paper, or put hand to keyboard, and write. Literally just start writing down anything you are thinking about. The mere act of writing down your thoughts will be healing and cathartic.

Part of my career is professional writing, but there is a difference between that and personal writing. After my breakup went down, all these emotions were going through my head, and I so very much wanted to purge those thoughts. I wrote in a journal. I wrote on my computer. I wrote in the Notes app on my iPad, on legal pads, on Post-its, or even on random scraps of paper lying around my office or home. To this day, I still write randomly all over the place. It gets my thoughts out of my head for good. After a breakup, there is a lot of stuff swimming around in your mind, some of which you can continuously talk about with your family and friends. But there are always those private things you want to keep to yourself. Use your solitude wisely and start writing.

The cool thing about journal writing is it becomes an exercise in being completely in the moment with your feelings. Also, being with yourself and writing, rather than having to fill the time in some other way, will relieve some of the pressure to always have something to do. Your something to do will be writing and healing. Although my musings became a book, you are more than likely not going for that goal, so cut yourself some slack. You're not writing a term paper or a cover letter for a job. Your words don't even have to make sense. They're merely your thoughts at the moment. It's a vulnerable task, for sure, but getting it out on paper or on your computer will bring you peace of mind. Journaling lets you express yourself without judgment from other people. Write down whatever you are feeling at the moment, but try to not reread what you wrote—just keep on writing and writing and don't go back. Sometimes you might feel the need to crumple up what you write and throw it out. If you feel so inclined, get rid of it. If you have a fireplace, burn it. If you have a shredder, shred it. It will feel like you are shedding pounds of emotional baggage in the process.

A second cathartic writing exercise is to write down three things you are grateful for each day. Move on to writing for a few minutes daily about one positive experience you had over the past twenty-four hours. As for *those* golden nuggets of wisdom, I'd say don't throw them out. You'll want to revisit those inspiring lists from time to time because rereading those words will empower you.

Another way to feel good is to write down *other people's sayings* on healing and put them up on your wall. Hang a bulletin board or some type of picture holder you can attach pieces of paper to somewhere in your home where you'll pass it every day. What will make that experience enjoyable during an otherwise horrific time is the fact that certain words, phrases, and quotes will make you feel better whenever you read them. New thoughts and a brighter outlook are there for the taking; you just have to create them. By writing down and hanging up words and quotes that *make* you feel good, you *will* feel good. Some quotes will make you smile and some will make you cry, but they will all help you start the process of surviving your broken heart. In the beginning, my board was filled with quotes and movie lines about survival. Many months after that, the quotes were not so dire, but rather about love, hope, and inspiration. I didn't plan it that way; it's just how the natural evolution of my healing took place. Here are some keepers that should fill your soul with love, if not inspiration, for awesome things to come.

To lose patience is to lose the battle.
—Mahatma Gandhi

I believe that everything happens for a reason. People change so that you can learn to let go, things go wrong so that you appreciate them when they're right, you believe lies so you eventually learn to trust no one but yourself, and sometimes good things fall apart so better things can fall together.

—Anonymous

You don't have to see the whole staircase, just take the first step.
—Martin Luther King, Jr.

It's astounding how well things work when we stop resisting or insisting.

—Mike Dooley

There are far, far better things ahead than any we leave behind.
—C.S. Lewis

You can't start reading the next chapter of your life if you keep rereading the last one.

—Anonymous

Have patience. Wait until the mud settles and the water is clear. Remain unmoving until right action arises by itself.
—Lao Tzu

Do not let the behavior of others destroy your inner peace.
—Dalai Lama

People think a soul mate is your perfect fit, and that's what everyone wants. But a true soul mate is a mirror, the person who shows you everything that is holding you back, the person who brings you to your own attention so you can change your life. A true soul mate is probably the most important person you'll ever meet, because they tear down your walls and smack you awake. But to live with a soul mate forever? Nah. Too painful. Soul mates, they come into your life just to reveal another layer of yourself to you, and then leave. A soul mates purpose is to shake you up, tear apart your ego a little bit, show you your obstacles and addictions, break your heart open so new light can get in, make you so desperate and out of control that you have to transform your life, then introduce you to your spiritual master.

—**Elizabeth Gilbert**

When love is not madness it is not love.
—**Pedro Calderón de la Barca**

The course of true love never did run smooth.
—**William Shakespeare**

How lucky I am to have something that makes saying goodbye so hard.

—**A.A. Milne**

And if you haven't yet read or heard the 2005 Stanford commencement address given by Steve Jobs, do it now. Look it up online, or better yet watch it on YouTube. This legend's message will change your life. Mountains will be moved. Breakup or not. Here's a sample from it:

You can't connect the dots looking forward; you can only connect them looking backwards. So you have to trust that the dots will somehow connect in your future. You have to trust in something—your gut, destiny, life, karma, whatever. Because believing that the dots will connect down the road will give you the confidence to follow your heart, even when it leads you off the well-worn path. And that will make all the difference.

YOUR TURN: Pick up a pen or pencil and start writing. If you'd rather type on your computer, that works too. Also start collecting quotes from every book, movie, and TV show you've ever come across. And read them.

HIT THE COUCH

My soul definitely needed more than chicken soup to solve what I was going through after my breakup. You too may have amazing friends and family that will listen to you cry and moan about how depressed you are, why things didn't work out the way they were *supposed* to, and all the other sad stories you have. But there is going to come a time when your friends and family are not going to want to hear it anymore. It's not that they don't love you, because they do; they've just run out of things to say to you to make you feel better. They are not professionals.

That's where psychotherapy comes in. Therapy is a touchy subject. The word comes with so many judgments. You say the word therapy and all of a sudden, there is something wrong with you and you're insane, need to be committed. You must have issues that no one else has. We're all so into talking about the overall health care issue, yet when it comes to the mental part of that equation, people get squeamish. Why?

Everybody needs a mental tune-up. And if you say you are the exception and don't need a mental tune-up, then you definitely need one more than anybody.

Not only is therapy a place where you can get out all your anger and sadness while you are going through a breakup, but also if you get a really good therapist you can start to analyze behavioral patterns in your past relationship that didn't work for you and how you can possibly go about your next relationship in a different, more productive way. I got a head start on therapy when I started noticing red flags between Mr. My Big and me the first time around. Friends suggested I go see a therapist and so I did, even though I had never been to one in my life. I did like the idea of spilling my guts to a complete stranger. There is something about a wise and educated person, unattached to you or to the outcome, helping you through a difficult situation that's kind of cool. It brings clarity to your situation. The tough part may be actually following through with what you discuss during your sessions. You won't have your therapist's hand to hold out there in the world.

The odd thing about therapy, though, if you're just going because some guy dumped you and you have a broken heart, is your sessions may leave you a little more confused than when you got there. If you really are committed to the process of therapy and want to stay in therapy for the long haul, then I'd say go for it. If you have the money and want to vent for 60 minutes once or maybe twice a week to gain a bit of perspective on your situation, and you're willing to listen to what the therapist has to say, do it. Jump on the therapy bandwagon.

But just to get out your feelings and cry a lot to a therapist about the guy you miss—I'm not sold on the idea. If you have the extra cash and are curious, sure, try it. But the whole idea of having an appointment for one hour during the week where you shed some emotional baggage stemming from your breakup, only to have his or her attention turn off when you leave with this "now what do I do feeling," doesn't seem worth it.

Remember though, what you're going through is rarely about the story. If you do see a therapist, you'll see how fast you get off the story of "what he did to you," and move on to working on *you*. That's what it is all about. Most of your thought patterns and behaviors stem from your early life. Your behaviors and thought patterns did not begin when this man walked out of your life, and they certainly won't end when a new man walks in. Changing behaviors and patterns, learning how to make self-honoring choices, takes discipline and a lot of practice. Having someone to guide you through that can change your life, if you're willing to stay the course. I had to really surrender to the fact that life sometimes doesn't work out exactly as we plan or hope and that adaptation to change is crucial. That's why I believe I held on so tightly to that relationship. I always assumed I would replicate my kind of happy, normal family life I grew up with. Coming to terms with the fact that I wasn't going to have all of that *exactly* when I wanted it was a tough pill to swallow. Acceptance of *what is* has always been a weakness. We all have weaknesses.

And here's the secret no one will tell you about therapy. While therapists are awesome at guiding you to the answer, this therapist of yours is really being paid so *you* can figure out the answers yourself. Yeah, we really can be our own counselors. Deep inside us, we know the answers. *You know* you have all the answers. It's that gut feeling you always have. It's that voice inside your head that steps in urging you to go the other way. It just becomes a matter of if you're willing to listen to your inner counselor.

If there's something *deeper* going on inside and you need an actual prescription for medication, that's where a psychiatrist comes into play. We tackle drugs (and alcohol) later in the book. Most therapists and psychiatrists take insurance. If you think this is the right path for you to take, you can find one in your plan and save some money. It doesn't have to cost a ton of cash to get help.

What I do know is change is really hard. It's crippling sometimes. If a professional can help ease some of the burden with tools and techniques to better help you through change, embrace it.

 YOUR TURN: Talk to your close friends or a doctor and go find a good therapist. Try a few out if you have to. Just find the right fit for you.

STAY BUSY

Mike Babcock, the coach of the Detroit Red Wings and the Canadian Olympic hockey team, once said of his team in the race for the Stanley Cup playoffs: "Do good things, and good things will happen." For a hockey coach, Babcock is a genius with words, and this quote still resonates with me to this day. It's a good quote for a sports team having a tough go at it and also for someone going through a breakup or rough patch because it illustrates that all you can do is do your best and let the universe catch up with you.

Bad things happen to good people. Actually, bad things happen to everyone. At the end of the day, it's about how you react to the setback. So how are you going to react to your breakup? My advice: stay busy. It can be dinner out, a trip, scheduling a class at the gym, going out dancing with your girlfriends, a new project at work, or even a television binge. Start with the first season of a show and watch it through the series finale if you want. It passes the time well, and you can stay home all you want. At some point, however, you need to leave the house and figure out what else you can do with your time. Whatever you are thinking about doing, have a plan. Making a plan gives you something to look forward to instead of walking aimlessly through your days and nights.

A tough part of picking up the pieces once a relationship is over is the abrupt end to the momentum you had going with that other person. Truth: since the man you thought you were spending the rest of your life with is no longer *in* your life, your everyday routine *is* going to change. Your daily rituals consisted of having a partner to walk through life with, and when that stops, it almost becomes like, now what do I do? The ultimate goal of this post-breakup period is to detach from your ex and to regain your independence. This step is a reprogramming of your life.

You're single now. As much as you may want to fight this fact, it's here and you're going to have to face this reality at some point. The key is not to hide away and spend your time staring at the walls by yourself in your house *forever*. It is another truth that being single in your twenties is night and day from being single in your thirties. Your friends now may be in relationships, your workload may be a bit more demanding and focused, and you certainly won't be going out hard-core as you may have back in the day. It is pretty tough to switch gears and change up your life in one week, let alone one month, but little by little you will be able to figure out new ways to go about your day on your own. Find a routine and stick with it, which will give you balance in your life.

It's a fact that post-breakup life does look different than your life before the breakup. One thing you may find is that you're not going to want to socialize with large groups of people. I know I had a lot of trouble getting back into the swing of things in big gatherings. The thought of it gave me anxiety. For a very long time, I would only feel comfortable having dinner one-on-one with friends or a very small group of people; in the beginning that is exactly where you need to be. Don't rush the process. You'll get back out there among the masses in time.

What is your day supposed to look like now, considering your day had been completely immersed in someone else's? My someone else took up a lot of my time and energy, and not always in a productive way. In time, I found it so freeing to not have Mr. My Big in my life because my time wasn't going toward worrying about his behavior. Being in a relationship with someone who was so deceptive was exhausting, and only after I was out of that relationship did I experience the relief of not having that time-sucking anxiety in my life anymore. Now it was time to get my life back, which included restarting all the activities I love to do and that make me shine. I was busy at work all day, busy at the gym in the early evening, and made plans every single night to keep my mind occupied.

Going all out at work gave me such satisfaction and a renewed sense of purpose. Staying busy for me included saying "yes" to every gig that came my way. I said yes to shoots and interviews on weekends, at night, super early in the morning. It didn't matter when I worked because I just wanted to stay busy, keep my brain active, and do what I love. Having all that free time was the best thing that could have happened to me and to my career. When I had shoots on a weekend I didn't have to worry about what I was going to do to keep myself occupied. I was doing what I was born to do. I can now say if it wasn't for my breakup, my career would never have reached the height that it has, because it was only after Mr. My Big and I ended for good that I really put in the hours necessary to make my dreams come true. Having to focus on me, not him, saved me.

But after a while I did start to crave more. That's when the idea of going back to school came into play. Using my newfound time wisely became almost a necessity, and I figured why not learn something new at the same time as trying to pass the time. I chose to go back to school to get my masters in spiritual psychology at University of Santa Monica, a private university in Southern California that offers a two-year, weekend-based master's program. USM has pioneered the integration of practical psychological techniques with empowering spiritual tools. I can certainly say the school and the program saved me. The curriculum seemed to fall into my world at just the right moment. Weirdly, I first learned about the program from Mr. My Big. He went through the program, as did Natasha. Mr. My Big went back to school during our relationship and I loved the textbooks he was bringing home. I began to crave the material.

As a student, I used examples from my own life to learn the psychology theories, techniques, and practices. I participated actively as a facilitator, client, and a neutral observer. Seeing and hearing life from all different types of perspectives was eye-opening, and I became a sponge. I wound up being on a path to healing one weekend a month for two years and getting a master's in the process. On the first day of school, when I was playing the role of the facilitator, I thought to myself, "Wow, every reporter should take this program." Just sitting in that chair, especially for two years, my listening and questioning skills became greater than any journalism experience could ever bring. Win-win.

You need to keep your mind very busy at this time, and I think there is no better way to do that than diving into new material, reading lots of books, writing papers, and getting another degree. Or getting your first degree if that's where you're at in life. One cool perk of going back to school is meeting new people. These fresh folks are going to help motivate you to be social again and to get out of the house for activities outside of school, too. If taking classes seems impossible because money is an issue, maybe your employer would pay for some or all of school.

There are scholarships out there for the taking, too. Don't *not* do it because of the money.

Between getting my master's, my TV writing job, my reporting and hosting work, writing my book, and trying to be semi-social, I was busy and finally started to feel balanced. My time was so full living my life that I didn't have time to think about my broken heart. And when I did think about it, enough good things were starting to pick up in my life that the gut-wrenching feeling from my breakup wasn't so gut-wrenching anymore.

This is the time of your life when you must keep moving forward. Remember, thought follows energy. Whatever you put your energy on, those are the thoughts that will follow, so by putting your energy toward a productive activity or loving yourself or family members, your thought pattern has only that way to go. You can choose to stay busy by thinking about your sad, unfortunate situation, but then you'll stay in that sad, unfortunate place. You can sit and be miserable for a longer period of time than you've already been grieving, or you can pick yourself up, *get busy*, and begin to heal. The faster you make the commitment to mend your broken heart, the faster you will begin to feel better.

Just after my deal was signed for this book to be published, I had a phone conversation with my 91-year-old grandmother my family calls Mama. We were talking about her health, if I was eating or not, the weather, if I booked my flights yet for Thanksgiving in Florida . . . you know the drill. And then I said, "Oh and Mama, guess what, I wrote a book and it's going to be published. Like, it'll be in bookstores and everything." She was so happy for me. I could really hear the joy in her voice, and the thing that stuck out the most was her saying to me, "You're always doing something good."

Mama passed away a few weeks after that conversation. It's a shame Mama never got to meet Coach Babcock. They shared a very similar outlook on life.

 YOUR TURN: What have you always wanted to do, study, or experience? Research local places where you can find what you are interested in doing. Go beyond your area and see what classes are offered online. Want to change jobs? Find a headhunter in your field, and check out job websites. Search and be curious.

FEEL THE PAIN

am not a doctor, nor do I pretend to be one. I certainly don't play one on TV. I'm not going to prescribe anything to you in this book and I'm not telling you to take certain things to make yourself feel better. I am simply sharing my story and what I did to heal my broken heart.

There is a big difference between self-medication and prescribed medication. I consider alcohol and recreational drugs sources of self-medication. Let's start with drinking. I know you're sad right now and the cocktails numb the pain. If you're already a drinker, after this breakup you might find yourself drinking a bit more than you expected. I was guilty of drinking a lot of alcohol after my breakup. I thought it was the best way to numb the pain. But that's all it does. It does not take it away and it certainly doesn't heal it. Alcohol is a depressant and it doesn't take a scientist to tell you that you should not be consuming a depressant when you're depressed. If you can do without the excessive drinking, then do it. I can almost guarantee you will feel better faster than if you're self-medicating with too many glasses (or bottles) of wine.

Your mind is in a fog right now, you're probably not thinking clearly, and you've no doubt lost weight so there's not much alcohol absorption going on either. And if you're driving, the last thing you want is a DUI arrest on top of a broken heart. That's not even mentioning how dangerous you are to other drivers on the road if you're not sober behind the wheel. You may be broken hearted, but don't be stupid. There's no excuse for stupidity.

As for drugs, I'm also not an expert on the subject. If you're doing anything illegal, you need more help than this book or I can give you and I urge you to find from a professional doctor immediately. After my breakup, I didn't try to escape by using drugs. Just wasn't my thing. You hear a lot of stories about people in their darkest moments turning to hard drugs, but I'm here to tell you it doesn't have to be that way. If the pain is that debilitating and you think hard drugs are the way out, please tell a family member or a friend and seek medical attention. There is help out there. If your heavy sadness feels like it just isn't going away on its own, medication to treat depression and insomnia may be something you need to look into. Again, I want to stress that I am not a doctor nor do I pretend to be. At a certain point, if there isn't a breakthrough in your breakup blues and you just can't get a handle on things, seeing a psychiatrist to prescribe a specific medication may be a route you need to take.

On that side of the spectrum, there are prescription medications, over-the-counter chill pills, and sleeping aids to help ease you through the day and night. Sleeping is so very important, and the older you get the more you need it. I break down emotionally when I don't sleep enough. But mastering the art of sleeping after a breakup is bloody impossible. Once your relationship comes to an end in all its hellish glory, all you no doubt really feel like doing is staying in bed and sleeping. Your body hurts. Your eyes are swollen shut. You are exhausted. You can't imagine getting out from underneath your big bulky covers to face the world, let alone move your body to do something productive with your time. I hear you. So don't. Give yourself permission to stay in bed and sulk and cry and stare at the ceiling.

But even though you're so comfortable in bed, underneath your down comforter, wearing the same worn out sweatpants and T-shirt you've been in for a week straight, a good night's sleep will be very hard to come by. Instead, waking up three times in the middle of the night with anxiety attacks can become the norm. It happened to me. I would wake up around three or four in the morning and the first thing I would think of was Mr. My Big. The second thing I would think of is that that he wasn't next to me. And then there was the third thing: that he was sleeping next to Natasha. Come on, God! Cut me some slack here. I remember even finding myself holding onto a pillow as if it were Mr. My Big and holding onto my thumb like I used to hold onto his thumb when we slept.

Learning to sleep alone, in your own bed, not in your man's bed, not next to your man, and not with all the warm, fuzzy things that come with sharing a bed, just plain sucks. So here you are, alone in that large bed of yours, not really knowing which side of the bed to sleep on now, and still having to get up in the morning and go to sleep at night. It may go on for many months. It may be time for help. In pill form. Again, consult a doctor. They could prescribe the sleep aid Ambien to you or tell you to take over the counter medication like Tylenol PM or melatonin. The best I can say here is eventually, this too shall pass. Uninterrupted sleep will be in your future. You've just got to get over this hump in a responsible way.

Then there is the fact that you need to get through the day. I never knew what anxiety was until it hit me. I sought help for that. A doctor prescribed something called Ativan that I would soon learn was an antianxiety medication. I had never heard of it before. I couldn't believe I was about to take a pill for anxiety. That alone gave me anxiety. But what it did was really take the edge off when I most needed it. The drug should be used responsibly, and again only when prescribed by a doctor. There's a reason you need a prescription for it. You can get addicted. You should only take prescription medication if you feel you are genuinely experiencing severe anxiety.

Bottom line: this time in your life is super tough. No one is saying it's not. So if there is responsible help out there to get you through the day and night, seek it out.

 YOUR TURN: Every day for the next week, keep track of your moods and sleeping patterns. If you are truly having a difficult time making it through the day or night, please see your doctor.

GET OUT OF DODGE

I started to use the title *Eat, Pray, Love* like a verb. After my breakup, when I wanted to travel somewhere, anywhere, I would say, "I'll Eat Pray Love it." My new saying and action symbolizes exactly what Elizabeth Gilbert wrote about in that best-selling book and what Julia Roberts portrayed in the movie. It means to be a woman who goes on a journey, solo, and sometimes if you're lucky you learn a bit about yourself on said journey. The movie came out in 2010, the year of my breakup, and I had read the book four years before that. By the time I wanted to take my own pilgrimage of sorts, I was totally feeling what she was selling.

If you want to keep any semblance of your sanity, travel. Staying in the same place where all your breakup drama went down may not help the situation. A change of scenery can help, however. By getting out of town, you are reprogramming your body and mind to do and experience different things, which will actually help flush the guy out of your system. For me, because Mr. My Big was merely a few blocks from my home, getting far away seemed like a really good idea. It would mean I couldn't just hop in my car and go see him. During my time away, anywhere I was other than that beach, I was forced by sheer distance to go at it without Mr. My Big, and it worked.

But leaving the familiar isn't easy to do. I sometimes struggled even getting on a plane to go visit my family on the East Coast. The very act of packing alone, going to the airport in a cab alone, waiting at the airport alone—it was hard. A lot of times after a breakup, it will feel easier and safer to stay in your own little world, but that won't help you heal and it *will* get stale very quickly. You will begin to crave something more than your usual surroundings, and it's always a good sign when you have the urge to grow and do.

First, figure out where you want to go and how you want to do it. Do you want to venture out into the world solo, meditate, and meet a medicine man in Bali or learn meditation in India like Liz did? Or do you want to keep it a bit closer to home and travel with friends? You decide what's within your reach and budget, but either way, you're going to get out of your rut and you're going to learn a hell of a lot about yourself. Done and done. One really easy way to pick a place to go is to ask all your close friends if any of them are taking business trips far away and if you can tag along. You can pay for your flight but share their hotel room. Maybe one of your friends is thinking about taking a trip somewhere but wants a travel buddy. Or maybe you are the type of gal who can run around the globe as a solo traveler. With a little creativity, the options are virtually limitless. Plus, all that trip planning will get your mind off him!

A friend of mine is from Morocco and I had always been extended an invitation to go back home with her. As it turned out, it was the same year as my breakup when I was invited again to her family's house right before the holidays. If that wasn't God giving me a swift kick in the ass, I don't know what was. Within weeks of that offer, my round-trip ticket to Casablanca was booked, first class to boot. I deserved it. Even as I wrote a portion of this chapter, I was sitting in the first class lounge at the Munich airport. Talk about post-breakup bliss! Flying first class internationally *is* all it's cracked up to be.

I went to Morocco about ten months after the big breakup. I was still in bad shape emotionally, but was quite eager for the new experience. Once I landed in Africa, it was quite apparent I was halfway around the world. Being in that country, with all its sounds, smells, colors, and tastes, was unlike anything I had ever experienced, and it really helped me not focus on my breakup every minute of the day. But I can't tell you I had the greatest experience being in Morocco. It was only after I returned from there that I was truly able to soak in what I had been through.

To this day, when people ask me about that trip I say I felt like Morocco was the angriest place I'd ever been. The cars seemed angry, the men seemed angry, the women seemed angry at the men, the air even felt angry. The wine, the tea, the fruits, and the meat felt really, really happy. Here's the thing I learned—all that anger I had toward Morocco really had nothing to do with the country itself. I was taught in graduate school, "Your outer experience is a reflection of your inner reality." There it was. I was angry about my breakup and angry with myself, so I looked at Morocco as one big angry country. I bet if I had gone to Disneyland, the so-called happiest place on earth, I'd have said Mickey Mouse was angry. I had wanted Morocco to save me and make it all better, but the truth of the matter was I had to save myself, and at that point in time, I just wasn't ready to allow that to happen. And so I took it out on the country.

I was simply manifesting my thoughts. While I was in these exotic cities such as Casablanca and Marrakech, things *really did* go downhill. Over breakfast on my first morning there, the friend I was traveling with revealed a secret to me about her own love life, something she had kept from me for our entire friendship. I was always led to believe her tears and agony over the course of our friendship were about her pending divorce, while the truth was, her grief was about a lover leaving her and ending their affair. While I didn't judge her, because who am I to judge given all the mistakes I have made, I felt duped for having been in the dark and more than slightly sad I wasn't trusted with that information. I was bummed she couldn't confide in me about her life while for all those years I had been spilling my guts out to her about Mr. My Big. Even though she did tell me I was the first person to learn this information, I lost a bit of trust in her—and trust was the one thing I needed desperately to start attracting back into my life. It was almost as if I was *still attracting* dishonesty into my world. Perhaps I still wasn't being honest with myself. I know now how I felt had nothing to do with her; she was merely reflecting back at me what I knew I needed and wanted in my life.

As the trip continued, I also started to get really sick, a deep burning in my chest mixed with laryngitis. So sick I thought I had pneumonia. Then, after sleeping on what I presumed was a bad bed in Marrakech, I sprained my back. Not kidding. The pain felt like lightning shooting up my spine. I couldn't even walk. And I had never hurt my back in my life. So there I was, coughing up a storm with barely any voice and the worst fire in my lungs, plus I wasn't able to stand without shooting pain traveling up my body. I wound up having to stay in bed for hours taking medication my friend's mom gave me. I was a mess.

Before returning to LA, I made a stop in NYC to see the family (my parents were visiting there at the same time). To not have them worry any more than they already were with me being in Africa, I called the day before I flew back to the states to tell them about all my ailments. "I need to go to the hospital or doctor's office straight from the airport, " I told them in my scratchy voice. "I'm really sick." And I did, and I was.

When I was back in the states, I learned I had sprained my SI joint—part of the lower back—for which the doctor gave me a prescription for Vicodin. The doctor also diagnosed me with a bad case of bronchitis, for which I got another set of pills.

All this time, I kept telling people, "Oh, the country literally rejected me being there." Only years later did I realize that angst had nothing to do with where I was. It doesn't matter if you're in the most beautiful spot on the planet or under the covers of your bed, your problems and how you approach them follow you wherever you go. And how I approached that friendship when I returned from Morocco was that I had decided to let it go. It just dissolved on its own. To this day, we've never talked about what happened, and I'm okay with that. People come into your life at various stages for a reason. They teach you things and then they leave. Like Mr. My Big. Look at all the knowledge this one friend being in my world taught me.

As long as you are not traveling to run away from your problems, and you are open to seeking new experiences and learning some life lessons along the way, a journey can become healing.

 YOUR TURN: List all the places you have ever wanted to go and all the places where you have friends. When you are ready, come back to this list. And then make a plan. Happy traveling!

BE INSPIRED BY OTHER SURVIVORS

P ractically everyone on the planet has experienced loss in some form or another, and yet when we're going through our own loss, we feel the most alone we've ever felt. All around us, in books, films, and music, the words of pain and suffering once felt by artists, musicians, and singers can be read and heard. Those artists survived it and lived to share it. What do they know that we don't? Nothing, actually. We all know the same thing, they just found a way to express it.

So many writers before me have attempted to crack the code on love and heartbreak. Many books are written on the matter. Like I've stressed before, there will come a time when you don't want to talk to your friends and family about your ex, so a great way to spend quiet time is by reading books on how to make yourself a better you. Yes, I am actually telling you to read other books besides the one you are reading right now because they will make you feel better, and it will help. After my breakup, I couldn't focus on much except, well, the breakup. I really did crave being inspired by other things besides the constant thought of Mr. My Big, but nothing was clicking. So I picked up self-improvement books and I just kept reading. Whatever books friends had on their bookshelves on self improvement, I read cover-to-cover. As I was reading, I would highlight, underline, and star all the parts that resonated with me with my trusty mechanical pencil. I remember I had to buy a lot of books when it was all said and done because I couldn't return all the marked-up books I had borrowed. What you'll come to find is you will start to talk your friends and family about the books you're reading and how they're working for you, instead of talking about the breakup.

There is something cathartic and grounding about reading self-help books during a dark time. It shows you that other people out there have been in your shoes. They survived and you will too. While you're reading this type of material, you will feel so much better, often regardless of what it's saying. That said, there is a lot of self-help stuff out there to go through, and while I did find some of the material really helpful to manage the pain, other books didn't help so much. Some advice told me to watch chick flicks with my girlfriends and make fun of all the guys. Not so much. Or stand up and say, "I am better than that guy, I deserve better!" That is true, but honestly at that time I wanted to tell half those authors where they could stick their rays of sunshine. You are not always going to forget about your ex in 30 days, even if a book is telling you that can happen. If you were in love with this person and your heart is broken, you will not forget him for the rest of your life. Down the road he's going to mean something totally different than he does now. But you will never forget him. And I wouldn't want you to.

Once I started grad school in spiritual psychology, the required reading was exactly the material I needed to help heal and it became ingrained in me. Not all of you are going to go and study psychology, but reading books in that field can help in times of crisis. Always keep a pencil handy while you're reading to underline and circle everything that holds meaning to you. These marks will be quite significant down the road when you're feeling blue. These are the books you will pick up and reread to pick yourself up.

What I definitely would tell you *not* to read: how about the wedding announcements in Sunday's style section of the *New York Times*, for starters. I absolutely love that part of the newspaper, but when trying to heal a broken heart, I would call it an unhealthy choice to peruse the paper looking at the happy pictures of recently married couples. Whatever city you live in and whichever paper you get, don't read any wedding announcements.

As for television viewing, bad choices include watching *Say Yes to the Dress* back to back for six hours, or any program pertaining to weddings, honeymoons, or babies. And you know all those reruns of *The Notebook*, *Pride & Prejudice*, and *Sense and Sensibility* that keep airing? Change the channel. Watching them thinking your man is going to come back and sweep you off your feet after time apart is a waste of time, because your reality does not look like that. Watching this stuff after a breakup is emotional suicide.

How about watching inspiring movies like all six *Rocky* movies. Watch them, study them, love them. They will teach you about perseverance in the face of adversity, how life is one big boxing ring and you must fight for yourself against all odds, and how ultimately it's not if you win or lose, it's whether you lead your life with heart and integrity that matters. A favorite quote of mine comes from the sixth movie in the series, *Rocky Balboa*. Rocky is at a point in his life where he's been through all the battles and has lost Adrian to cancer, and yet he's still standing, he's still surviving. He says, "You, me, or nobody is gonna hit as hard as life. But it ain't about how hard you hit. It's about how hard you can get hit and keep moving forward. How much you can take, and keep moving forward. That's how winning is done."

Then there's music. Countless songs have been written about love, breakups, and heartbreak, and most of the lyrics are about pain and suffering. Etta James knew it. Alanis Morissette got angry from it. Adele experienced it. John Mayer is always trying to figure it out. Taylor Swift makes a living off of it. Every note, each lyric, vibrates in our souls as if these songs were written just for us. Well those singers and songwriters *are* us. They're human and have experienced the same pain you are experiencing. For example, the day my book deal was ready to close with the publisher, I got a bit apprehensive. There was this overwhelming sense of fear that ran through me and said, "Don't do it," because I didn't want people to think I was still dwelling on this breakup. It had been so long. My thought process shifted after a conversation I had with my sister, who reminded me that when singers are explaining how they came up with a certain song or where lyrics came from, they always say they wrote that song when they were going through something traumatic in their life. All those artists and musicians aren't necessarily going through that very emotion anymore, but they were when they wrote the song. My sister told me that was like my book. It was at that moment I got it.

As a writer on *E! News* for the past ten years, I have come to know a lot about the love lives of celebrities. During an interview Britney Spears was giving about her eighth studio album, she told the reporter the inspiration for the songs on it was her split with her former fiancé, Jason. She said of the split, "They suck. Breakups suck, man. They do." Creativity was born from her pain like so many artists before her.

All that music you are listening to over and over again, whether it's Coldplay, Pink, or the Eagles, they've all been there and have lived to sing about it. Back in the day, I don't know how I would have gotten through those young love heartbreaks without Air Supply, Journey, Chicago, and REO Speedwagon. You give me a ballad, I probably cried over a boy to it. "Against All Odds" by Phil Collins. I think he wrote it for me. I had more cassette tapes labeled "love mix" than I did any other type of music. Nothing has changed as far as music is concerned. It still speaks to us when it comes to love and heartbreak, regardless of the artist, regardless of the song.

From tragedy comes art. It's cathartic for the artist, which in turn helps the listener. Keep listening, keep reading, keep watching. It helps with the healing.

 YOUR TURN: Borrow all the self-help books you can find on your friends' bookshelves. Go to the bookstore and buy all the titles that spark your interest. Go online and buy titles that tickle your fancy. Then cozy up on the couch and start reading. Not only will it pass the time, but you will also learn something about yourself. Watch heartfelt movies to inspire you. Listen to music that speaks to you.

GO COLD TURKEY
WITH YOUR EX

Let me tell you from experience: *any* communication with your ex after a painful breakup is not recommended. It's just never good. Of course, I'm talking about in-person contact, but in this day and age it's also about the texting, the sexting, the tweets, the Instagram pics, the emails, the IMs—whatever type of social media you're into. Any type of communication is toxic. Going cold turkey is probably the hardest thing you will ever have to do, but succeeding at it could very well be the greatest gift you give yourself.

Sex can keep two people together for way longer than they should be together, but it should not be mistaken for the other things necessary to keep two people together. Those things were probably missing in your relationship, which is no doubt what you are trying to cover up with all that makeup sex. What you're doing will mask the problem for a short while, but even great sex can't cover up the not-so-great parts of a relationship. And I bet you're telling your man that you can handle it, you won't get attached, and you understand what's going, but deep down you don't understand what's going on and you're hoping the sex will make him stay. The only thing it's doing is prolonging your pain. Save your dignity and stop.

After the initial split with Mr. My Big, when he and I were still hanging out, he wasn't my boyfriend anymore so I really should have gotten on with things. The getting on with things was always the toughest part. Instead I just got it on with him, and look how well that worked out. Mr. My Big and I were magnetic. Even when we tried to stay apart, we always found a way to get close to each other again. After the breakup, I would see him about once a week, usually at the gym. Then we'd cry and hold each other in the parking lot of the gym, talk on the phone on the way home from the gym, and schedule the next time we could see each other because it was too painful to separate. We'd IM each other at work and text in between. It was me that couldn't let go. My friends and family thought I was certifiable for continually going back to this guy, but he was my person. Mr. My Big was the person I went to for everything, professionally and personally. So after the breakup I had to find a way to go at it without him, and it was really hard, but I did it, very, very slowly. I'm telling you, you have to break apart or you will never move on.

People will tell you after a breakup to delete your ex's phone number and all their contact information from your phone immediately. I know some people who have done this and others who haven't. I did not, but if I had maybe the mess I kept getting myself into after we broke up wouldn't have dragged on for as long as it did. Seriously, if you delete his number, on the off chance he really needs to get in contact with you, he will find a way. If he broke up with you, the last thing you should be doing is reaching out to him anyway.

If you're meant to be back in each other's lives somewhere down the road (which is the exception, not the rule, so don't focus on that too much) you will find each other again. More importantly, he will find you. And listen, I know the whole deleting him from your life thing is brutal, but the other way probably isn't working, is it? *I wish* I took the delete advice back in the day.

Ladies, going back for more will not heal your heart. When you and your man break up and it is clearly over, just break up. Maintaining some type of hold on what you had will only make it that much harder to move on. I'm sure you've heard this before, but if you continue to keep this person in your life, you will never have that space open for someone new to come in. I hated hearing that from people. I wanted to scream, "But you don't understand!" Yeah, they did understand, and I had to learn the hard way. Allowing yourself the space to walk away from someone you loved very much will hurt like hell and will no doubt leave a big hole in your life. But after a breakup, that hole is *not* supposed to be filled with the person who just left it behind. He left it. Why would you want to give it back?

Staying in communication with Mr. My Big was beyond unhealthy. My mood always seemed to rely solely on him and how responsive he was to my text messages, IMs, and phone calls. If I didn't hear back for a while or he seemed distant in a text message, I would begin to stress out. Instead of wiping Mr. My Big's existence clean from my life, I would play a game. Seeing as the key to any new attempt at change is to make a new behavior a habit, I applied that theory to my communication with Mr. My Big. For example, I would say to myself, "Let's see how long I can go without texting him." It was huge if I made it one week, and once I made it one week I figured I could keep going. Until he contacted me, that is. Then, sadly, all bets were off. So, all our laughs, long nights, sweet texts, and inside jokes we shared *post-breakup* were not meant to be taken as him wanting to get back together with me? If I had just cut off all contact with him, maybe that whole song and dance wouldn't have dragged on for as long as it did.

I know it feels really good to hear your ex telling you "I miss you," and "I love you," and "You're really the one I want to be with," but he is not your guy anymore. If he does want to be back in your fold, let him prove it. Most likely, that little bit of pleasure you get from those few words over a text message will cause you more harm in the end. If you still want to see/talk/have sex with your ex, let's discuss how he broke up with you. Maybe remembering that terrific moment in your life will make you never want to see/talk/have sex with him again.

Did he disappear on you? Did he fall off the face of the earth without telling you where he was going? Maybe you guys were dating for a couple of weeks, or maybe even a couple of months, and you thought, "Wow, this could be the guy." Well, when days turned into weeks and you hadn't heard from him, maybe you figured out he wasn't coming back but the rejection still killed you. To this day, it's been radio silence. Waiting for a text or phone call that will never come is brutal. You are worth enough to have the "we have to break up" conversation.

Instead of becoming a ghost in your world, maybe he pulled away really, really slowly. Strung you along for a really, really long time. Maybe he didn't text as often as he had in the past. Maybe he started to make other plans on the days and nights usually reserved for you. However he backed away while still keeping some semblance of a presence, it drove you absolutely crazy. So great, both of you were too scared to pull the plug so it dragged on in ugly, dark, murky waters for longer than it should have. He ultimately was so far gone you just figured it was over, so great, you had no closure. I'm sure that felt really good, too.

Or did he cheat on you? Did you catch him? Did he lie about it? Maybe he cheated and you took him back. Maybe he cheated a lot and you took him back, a lot. This type of guy is selfish and if this was your guy, he had the problem, not you. Your problem was just taking him back. And taking him back. And taking him back.

Maybe your relationship dragged on forever while he went back and forth between you and someone else and you weren't strong enough to walk away. After the big breakup conversation the two of you no doubt had, he let you sleep over all the time and spend time with him at home and around your neighborhood. You maybe thought this type of behavior would make him stay with you, even though you'd bawl your eyes out because he was still so distant afterward. Maybe he told you what he thought would make you hang around longer just so *he* didn't feel the sting of loneliness, when really he had no plans for you to be in his life long term. Any scenario after it drags on like this and he doesn't end up with you will be devastating.

Even if he was the ultimate gentleman and ended the relationship with class by actually being honest with you, saying he doesn't see a future with you and he doesn't want to waste your time, do you still want him back after he told you he essentially doesn't want to marry you? He broke up with you because he doesn't see you as his wife. I don't think you want to be that person. Do you?

If any of these scenarios sound familiar, I'm not sure why you'd want any of these guys back in your life. Do you really want to experience all that heartache and drama again? You decide. If he's The One, he'll come back on his own. He won't want to let you go.

I'm not saying going cold turkey is the easiest task to master, but it is the ideal way to start healing your broken heart. Gather your strength and go for it. I am smart enough to know even the strongest woman in the world may not be able to pull it off. You've spent part of your life with someone. It's going to be tough. But, day by day, it will get easier.

You *may* one day find yourself on friendly terms with your ex, but most likely it won't be right after he breaks your heart. Every story is different. I'm just saying once you guys have gone through a breakup, take time away from each other. Give each other space. The only way to separate yourself from him may be to just delete him from your life for a while.

P.S.—Don't even think of doing drive-bys. If your ex-boyfriend sees you driving by his house at *any* hour of the day or night, the last thing he is going to be thinking is, "Oh, I miss her. Why don't I invite her in and hold her all night long?"

 YOUR TURN: Delete your ex's contact information. Force yourself to take alternate routes away from his house if you're near him. Do not sleep with him after you've broken up. Try really, really hard on this one.

BE AVAILABLE

Once your man is gone, the mere thought of being with *another* man may be unthinkable. You may just be anti-guy. All you may have energy to do is go to work, see some friends, and maybe travel a bit. The furthest thing from your mind will be talking to another man, let alone going out with one. I understand if you are not ready to date yet. That is okay. Don't let anyone pressure you to do anything you don't feel like doing, because there are going to be people who tell you the fastest way to get over one guy is to get with another. I didn't buy it, and you don't have to either if you don't want to. God bless some of my dear girlfriends who were able to date and have sex right after their breakups. What were they drinking that I wasn't? Well, I know what they were drinking, but it still didn't help my cause.

I couldn't even have conceived of being with someone else at that time, even though many men tried. Each week and month that went by, my friends couldn't believe who I had become. I couldn't believe it either. The fact that I was still involved with Mr. My Big after our breakup made it super tough to get close to anyone else. I hung out with a bunch of other guys and went out on dates, but looking back I feel they were just fillers for the moment. They were something to help pass the time. If you're one of those guys and you're reading my book, my apologies.

For example, a guy I met at some gathering I dragged myself to asked me out for coffee. It was only a few months after the breakup, and I didn't want to go. But someone once had advised me to "fake it till you make it," so I decided to heed that advice and go. But I want you to read something I wrote on my BlackBerry while I was waiting for the guy to show up:

> *Don't want to do this. I miss M———. I just want to be with him. What the f—k am I doing right now? And it's only coffee!!?? The only reason I am having coffee with this person is because "they" say it's what I have to do. What does this feel like? Almost like being made to take my wheezing medicine when I was young. Awful.*

I shared that excerpt with you so you can see that it will suck and it won't feel good, *at first*. But, I promise there will come a time when you are going to want companionship again. It just won't be right away. I wouldn't recommend forcing yourself to go out on dates if you don't think you're ready. You will absolutely know in your heart if and when you want to meet someone new. What has worked for others (dating, meeting new guys, flirting, random sleepovers, one-night stands) may not work for you after your breakup, and it will probably be the most organic thing you'll ever do. Spending time by yourself and really looking at who you are is healthy. It's time to reassess. Out with the old (literally) and in with the new (when you're ready). But it did take what felt like forever to get rid of the old, and I can now say that is why it took me so long to find something new.

One of the main reasons I couldn't grapple with the idea of being with another man, or even liking another man, was my continued attachment to Mr. My Big. Every time I went back to Mr. My Big, even when he was with Natasha, I was closing myself off to meeting anyone else. It's true when you keep someone on the backburner of your life, it really does prevent you from opening yourself up completely to someone new. By keeping that charade up, I set myself back by months in the moving-on process. Each time I went back, I had that many more weeks added to my time of attempting to get over him. It was an excruciating cycle. This is where the benefits of going cold turkey really begin to materialize.

It was a good six months after the last time I was with Mr. My Big before I considered flirting or going out with another guy. I just didn't have it in me before that. Now, looking back, I have such compassion for that girl who just wasn't strong enough to move on and get on with her life. It's okay, because it took going through all that pain to get my strength back and my dating legs back. I don't believe the quickest way to get over a man is to get a new man, because what that doesn't do is get you back to who you were *without* a man attached at your hip. You want to go into a relationship as whole as possible, and going right back into another partnership so quickly after the last one could mean you're rebounding or you're lonely for any company you can get. Although, if you're reading this and you met the man you married right after a really bad breakup, congratulations! You should write a book!

Once Mr. My Big and Natasha's wedding happened, my strength really kicked in. It was game on. My first guy after the drought wound up being a Broadway star whom I interviewed backstage. From then on, I wound up meeting and dating some of the most incredible, talented men I have ever known in my life. By that time, I was really and truly over Mr. My Big and the breakup. I had completely come into who I was at the most authentic level, and without even trying I was radiating that into the world and at these men. It felt redemptive.

While I have never tried Internet dating, some people I know swear by it. It seems like the world is finding love online. I've always been more of the let things happen organically type of person, and that's how I always met my boyfriends, so I kept along that same pattern. I don't want to talk you out of Internet dating, because it could work for you. Online dating is not for me, but a lot of people do it, so you can sign up and create a dating profile just to see where it takes you.

But if you find yourself moving from one relationship to the next without having any luck, stop yourself to see if there's a pattern to the men you're dating and, furthermore, how you're coping with the breakups. You want to have better judgment next time you dip your toes into the dating world, and now is the time to get that compass straight. Instead of jumping back into another relationship, perhaps you need to take more time by yourself to explore who you are and understand why you would stay in something that wasn't right instead of being on your own. I know *I* needed to be by myself for a time rather than with another man to identify what type of guy I really wanted and to pledge to myself not to settle until I found someone who possessed those special *and honorable* qualities.

When I knew I was ready to start dating again, I told my friends and coworkers that I was ready to be set up. To this day, though, only one of my friends has tried to set me up. Some other people's excuses were, "We don't know anyone good enough for you," or "I don't know any single guys," or even "I don't think you're ready, so why would I want to set you up with one of my friends only to have his heart broken?" Yeah, all of them were classics, but they were right. I wasn't ready. But at least I was being proactive.

So, when someone tells you to get back on the horse, you don't have to listen. You may not find someone you want to ride off into the sunset with right away, and that's cool. You are trying to sort out a mess of emotions right now, and waiting around for someone to help you clean up that mess doesn't seem, to me, like the wise path. It's your responsibility, not someone else's. Once you get your confidence back, anything can happen. Even, perhaps, true love. But it starts with being available.

 YOUR TURN: Tell everyone you know that you are available and looking. You have nothing to lose and you never know. Write down all the qualities you are looking for in a partner. Once it's complete, hang it up on your wall. This puts your request out into the universe. In the end, that's all you can really do. And when all else fails, just be you. The new guy will come around when you're ready.

CREATE YOUR HOME

You lived with your significant other, or you slept in each other's homes every night. You cooked meals together in his kitchen. You bought groceries for his fridge. You shared closet space. You mixed his laundry with yours. Your bathroom supplies took over his bathroom. Brushing your teeth together at night was the highlight of your day. Your razor was in his shower. The alarm clock was set for both of your wake-up times.

You shared a home with someone and now that someone, and the home you once shared, are no more. Creating *your* home, *your* space, *your* surroundings, after a breakup is a crucial step in the process of healing your broken heart. I'd actually say try to do this step as soon as possible—once you've gotten through the truly dire moments after the split—because having a place to call home, one that brings you peace, calm, and a bit of serenity, will become a beautiful base for you to do your inner work while you are healing.

I remember the morning inside Mr. My Big's home when we broke up like it was yesterday. Every weekday morning before he left for work, he'd sit on the edge of the bed in a sweet way while I was half asleep, and I would curl up into his lap, slightly whining in a cute, still sleepy voice, telling him I didn't want him to leave. That was the routine every morning, and that was scene the moment we broke up, too, although there was no curling up in his lap that time. I woke up to him sitting on the side of the bed next to me with his *other face*: a boyish grin turned upside down mixed with sad, dark brown puppy-dog eyes that always had something bad to say. Bomb. Dropped.

Thomas Jefferson once said, "Nothing gives one person so much advantage over another as to remain cool and unruffled under all circumstances." Well, after that breakup conversation, this was the moment I had to remain cool in order to get all my stuff out of there in the quickest way possible. And it was hard. Mr. My Big sat on the floor, back against the wall, staring into space, looking like someone had just killed his cat. I'm not sure what he was thinking at the time, but he didn't offer to help me pack up my stuff, nor did I ask him to. I was in a mad rush to clean house. I had almost half my life in that place. I called it dignity in garbage bags—and those many, many garbage bags then had to make their way back to my old apartment. An apartment I barely lived in and now had to go back to. The reality of the situation didn't hit me right away. You have no idea what hit you until you're sitting in your old place a few days later with boxes and bags surrounding you.

Going back to my old apartment after essentially living full time with my guy was lonely and uncomfortable. I didn't want to sleep in the bedroom, so I slept on the couch for weeks. I had never really slept in that bed, and I surely wasn't about to start then. I hate with a passion sharing walls and hearing people on the other side, and that's exactly what I had to go back to in that apartment. Even though it had an ocean view and was a block from the beach, going back there felt like I was going back in time, and I needed to move forward. I stayed in that apartment for only a few more months, until I had figured out three things: I needed change big time, a move would be major change, and I had always wanted to live in a house. Thus began my search for the perfect beach house.

The process of looking for a cute little place on the beach was not an easy task, mind you, but since I was financially in a position to do it, I made it into my little project. Searching for that house kept me very busy. Remember the seventh step: stay busy. Every day after work I would set up a couple of appointments to see houses at the beach. Most of them didn't work; they were either too expensive or not nice enough. But what all that looking did was solidify what I *did* want. I loved hardwood floors, a fireplace, a modern kitchen, and in-house laundry. By the time I saw the house that eventually became the one I live in now, I knew instantly it was mine. And I took it in that moment.

Then came the decorating, the furniture placement and all those finishing touches. The house became my Zen palace, and it wound up being the perfect place for me to heal. I loved inviting people over for wine and conversation by the fireplace. Redecorating, creating your own space with new things and new energy, will do wonders for your psyche. You're rebuilding your life, and one of the best ways to do that is rebuilding a home and setting it up. You need a place to recharge. This is that place. It's for you and only you. And trust me, you will have visitors eventually. You just have to start inviting them over.

While I chose to stay in the same neighborhood after my breakup, sometimes moving to another area in your city, or even to another state, could just be what you need to flush this guy out of your system. I know women who have done both. Starting over in a new place can do wonders for your life. All it takes is the courage to decide where you want to go and to then move confidently in that direction. Maybe it's time to move closer to where your family lives, or maybe this is the time for you to live out a dream of moving to a certain city in the world. Now could be the time you seek out a new job you want in another state. Seize this golden opportunity. Since only you know what is really a conceivable city or town, you can dream big, but the time will come for reality. Maybe a move down the block? Across town? A new state? Maybe stay in your home and redecorate? Guess what? It's your time to decide what you want.

And, of course, with long-term relationships comes a lot of stuff—the pictures, the videos, the stuffed animals, the shared furniture, the candle he gave you that you haven't burned yet, the cards he wrote you with the sweet messages in them, his broken-in college T-shirt or the sports jersey he got you with his hockey number and your nickname on the back of it. Every relationship comes with stuff. You basically have two options here: put all these physical reminders of him either into storage or into the garbage. Do not put them on display in your new space. This will help you build a home for you and only you. Especially when it's time to invite a new guy over to your place; the last thing he needs to see is a picture of you and your ex-boyfriend staring down at him.

Fresh space. Fresh outlook. Fresh start.

 YOUR TURN: Write down all the things you want in a new home, from furniture to your decorating style. Now, write down all the places you want to live. Figure out what works best for you and begin the process of moving on.

LAY LOW, SOLO

Get comfortable being alone in the present. It's the only way to not be alone in the future.

One of the greatest lessons you will take away from a breakup is learning how to be alone. You must learn how to be alone even if you don't like to. I want you to now learn how to enjoy your own company and not be dependent on someone else for companionship, especially your ex. There is a massive void going on in your world right now, and you must fill it all by yourself, which means not running into another man's arms and especially not trying to wiggle your way back into your former significant other's bed. There is a good chance you will relapse; if and when you do, don't beat yourself up about it. Just get it out of your system and then get him out of your life. In the beginning, being single, not part of a couple, will no doubt feel uncomfortable, but that doesn't mean trying to force your man to get back together by any means possible. Learning to lay low solo takes courage and patience, but there is no other way. You've got to go through it, not around it.

I am not saying be alone for the rest of your life. I actually think single women who say they don't need a man and they're happy being without someone aren't, for the most part, being truthful with themselves. I'd much rather be in a relationship than be single, but I'd never trade the time I took after my breakup for anything, because it was during those months that I got back to me. Like the wise sage Carrie Bradshaw once said, "The loneliness is palpable." After a breakup, the empty space in your life will be as glaring as it ever will be, but this is not the time to retreat into self-loathing. It's time to figure out how to be comfortable with just you. Running around life solo, alone, does take a certain amount of confidence and self-awareness, but it's not that hard. If you can't hang out with yourself, why would a man want to hang out with you?

But there is a huge difference between being alone and being lonely. Being alone is basic. It's when you're not with other people but you don't have that empty, something-is-missing feeling. It's being okay eating out at a table for one with a good book. It's enjoying your own company whether you are curled up on the couch or walking down the street. Loneliness, on the other hand, is having that hollow feeling inside and craving the presence of another person. It's looking at that table set for one and wanting it set for two. It's wishing there were two of you sitting on the couch or walking down the street so you had someone to share the experience with.

Months after your breakup, and months after your friends and family have taken care of you, and months after you've settled into a comfortable flow in life, you will find that you're spending a lot of time by yourself. You could be doing any of the things I've advised so far—journaling, traveling, reading, or visiting family. During that time, there will come a moment when you all a sudden realize that you are okay by yourself, that it's okay to go at it alone for the time being. It's during this time that you're getting your world back on track, going after the things you want to do, and learning to love yourself the best way you know how. You're doing *you*. When the time is right, you will be able to bring a fresh new you to the table for a new guy to fall in love with. Let the universe catch up with you. Starting over, change: it's so damn hard but, in some cases, so brutally necessary.

If you don't want to go out, quality "me time" at home is always a good option. Sit in the shower and steam. Take a bath. Light candles, put on soft music, and immerse yourself in hot water and vanilla-scented bubbles. Meditate. If you don't know how, just sit in stillness and try to clear your mind. Keep it clear and calm for a few minutes. Take deep breaths. And now you're meditating. Do it every day for five minutes and you'll feel calmer. Make coffee in the morning and drink it one sip at a time. Repeat that ritual at night with a pot of tea.

Another way to entertain yourself at home is Netflix or video on demand. Talk about a great way never to leave your house, stay in sweats all day and all night, never have to do your hair or put on makeup, and, at that rate, not even have to shower. It's a party for one. It's your life, and right now you get to run it as you see fit. Be careful, though, not to watch so much television that it becomes an alternative to socializing. If and when you are craving a trip out of the house solo, there are quite a few options to try out. I've created a short list of activities to do when not a friend is in sight, and when you don't really want a friend in sight anyway.

Go to the movies. I never really was a fan of sitting in a dark movie theater alone, but it's kind of cool not having to check in with anyone about what movie they want to see, what time they want to go, and what they thought of the film. It's all on your own time. It's empowering. When I go back to New York City, my favorite thing to do, single or not, is to go to the movies by myself at the Lincoln Center theater on the Upper West Side. I absolutely love it. Try it in your hometown and see how it feels. Do it once and the fear goes away.

Take yourself shopping. There's something to be said about looking at clothing, jewelry, or any tangible item, making a decision that you like it, and deciding you would like to have it. The person who invented the phrase "retail therapy" knew what they were talking about. Even running a simple errand like grocery shopping to buy food can make you feel a bit normal again.

Go for a long, long drive. Road trips can be so much fun. There is a stark beauty to a long paved road ahead of you and a destination in sight. So many adventures could occur while you're behind the wheel. The key for long stretches on the road is to have a solid playlist, too. Good music will get you very far in life, and without it, the air can seem pretty dull. So turn up the tunes and take to the road. You could even find a beautiful hike somewhere. Now that's something to leave your house for.

Cut out the self-pity, cut your losses, and stop playing victim. It's time to stop giving power to the person who broke your heart and take it back for yourself.

 YOUR TURN: Start by trying to be alone for one day and see what happens. One day will turn into two, then three . . .

FIND YOUR FUN

Fun isn't something that happens overnight. Your heart will not heal, and the pain will not completely disappear in a few days, let alone in a month. Maybe it will take two or three. Maybe four or five. You're not going to feel like laughing or playing for a while, and that is quite natural. The good news is you will not stay in your anti-fun funk forever. There's a reason this step is in the middle of the book and not the beginning. I don't expect you to be the life of the party when your life doesn't look like it did a week ago.

The key is to create fun in your life gradually. Do something that could be perceived as fun, either by yourself or with a group of people, maybe even bitch and moan your way through it, and at some point you'll find yourself with a smile on your face. When people start inviting you out to do things, just say yes. Go. Go have fun with your friends. Even if you're not having fun while you're there, you might pick up on some of the enjoyment and store the good vibes for later. This step is combining the earlier steps of never be alone, stay busy, and lay low, solo. Now you're making sure there is some fun thrown into the mix.

In the wake of a breakup, people often do crazy things, like skydive, move abroad, or cut their hair or dye it a wild color. For me, after the running wild stage of trying to fill every moment with some sort of stimulation, all I wanted to do was drink wine with my girlfriends, take a walk on the path by the beach, babysit my friend's kids, or travel across the country to sit and watch TV on my family's couch. Yes, those things are enjoyable to me, but that's not the type of fun I'm talking about here. For the purposes of this chapter, I want you to think outside the box. Be adventurous. Be spontaneous. Be courageous. Do something fun you've always wanted to do but haven't done yet.

Take a bartending class. Join an adult sports league. Learn how to make wine. Learn how to sew. Start a blog. Volunteer at a shelter. Prep for a marathon. Go to a cooking class. Paint.

Find your fun.

One solo excursion I embarked on was trapeze school. I originally saw it on an episode of *Sex and the City*, and there was one in my city. It felt completely corny, but that's why I did it. It was an activity I never would have thought of doing in the past, it seemed like it *could* be fun, and even though I was not in the mood to have fun, I forced myself to go. I surprised myself. Just being up that high and flying through the air made me smile. The rush alone made me feel good. Whether or not you join the circus for the day or jump out of an airplane, the point is you will be concentrating on something else for a while, other than your ex and your sorrow. You'll be putting your energy into enjoying yourself. I'm not saying the trapeze is for everyone, but you get the idea. Partaking in any type of fun activity will be good for your well-being, as it will condition your brain to start thinking about other things.

There was one activity I did that didn't feel so good. I adore tennis—adore playing it, adore watching it. I even dated a professional tennis player for a minute post-breakup. Right after my split, I thought, oh wow, I have so much time on my hands, why don't I take tennis lessons now? Even though I had lessons growing up and was on the tennis team in junior high. But when I did join adult group tennis lessons, I felt like I was some old lady trying to keep herself busy. And while I was a young lady trying to keep myself busy, I just couldn't shake the feeling I wasn't in the right spot. It was almost like I was trying too hard to take my mind off my sadness. So that didn't work.

The takeaway from all the trial and error of finding fun things to do is that eventually you will find your match and it won't feel like you're just trying to fill time. You can also revisit old hobbies that used to make you smile. Remembering the things you once enjoyed and that you always put so much pride in will distract you from the heartache you're experiencing. The act of doing one of those activities will start to bring life back into your soul. Whatever things you once loved, you will love them again. Take one day at a time and maybe, just maybe, you will have fun one of those days. When you catch yourself laughing you'll know what I'm talking about.

Now, about those fun and exciting activities you did with your ex—yeah, that is *not* a good idea. No genius insight here when I tell you it is just not a wise choice to keep up the activities you did with your significant other right after the breakup. What better way to keep reminding yourself that your man is gone than by doing the things you did together, minus the guy? I know firsthand how the idea of doing your old fun things might make you feel better. But it doesn't. It will have the opposite effect.

For instance, Mr. My Big and I always went to hockey and baseball games together. It was our thing. I thought by continuing those activities with one of my friends right after the breakup, I would feel better. Oh, how wrong I was. Being in those spots was a total trigger for me. They were stark reminders of my trauma, which just caused anxiety and stress. I will right now admit that I have cried at professional baseball and hockey games. And I'm pretty sure that's not the reaction one is supposed to have while watching a live sporting event. That trigger didn't last too long, only a few months, and it's a good thing because I am a sports junkie.

Now that we're talking about it, don't even go to the restaurants and bars you went to with your ex. I did that too, for a while, because I really enjoyed talking to the bartender at one place we went every Thursday for years. I hated the thought of not being able to go there and drink anymore and not talking to one of our buddies. It was part of our week. But that's just what it was, part of "our" week, and there wasn't an "our" anymore. The universe had a funny way of taking care of business, because a few months after Mr. My Big and I broke up, this longstanding establishment closed forever. It had been in our neighborhood for about fifty years, but the place couldn't stay open anymore due to money issues. So it closed. Symbolic. My relationship was done and our place was done. I was forced to move on.

Having fun again means saying yes to invitations and saying yes to parties, but it also means having that whole "plus one" thing to deal with. When you're single and you get invited to an event, wedding, or dinner party with a plus one, it could trigger sad feelings about not having your built-in plus one anymore. Although, I actually think what's worse than getting the plus one to an event when you're single is *not* getting that plus one. At least with the plus one invitation, you now have the option of bringing someone, a friend or a crush, to an event and having a good time. So let me reiterate. If you get a plus one on an invitation, definitely, without a doubt, put on a dress, grab an able body, and go. If you don't get a plus one on the invitation, still go. You're more than likely to meet new people, have lots of interesting conversations, enjoy good food and wine, and maybe, just maybe, have a little fun.

YOUR TURN: What type of activity seems fun for you that you have never done? Find it locally, or even far away, and go do it. As much as what you used to do with your ex was fun, find new activities to make you smile or the old ones you gave up because you never had enough time. You have the time now.

DETAIL YOUR LIFE

When you put effort into how you look and in what manner you present yourself to others, you will be radiating good vibes. By putting your best foot forward, you are commanding respect, and people will notice in a very positive way. You detail your car, now it's time to detail your life.

Let's start at the top, with your hair. Making an appointment to have a stylist give you a haircut, change up your style, and spruce up or even change your color, will put a slight bounce back in your step. Just think, after you get that fabulous blowout, you don't have to wash your hair for days and you can continue to walk around looking and feeling fabulous even if you are faking it. Having your hair done will not make you get over your man any faster, but it will help *you* feel good for a moment. And little moments here and there add up to a lot of moments, which add up to all the time. For everyday hair issues, try to be presentable when you step out of your house. Untie your hair from that ratty old rubber band and let down your locks. Be free.

Put on an attitude of, you are doing just fine. Another manageable way to accomplish that is by cleaning yourself up for public outings. Not just by finally taking a shower, but by dressing to impress. Next time you have a party or a dinner to attend, wear something fabulous. Literally, get dressed. Take off your dingy sweats, remove your baseball hat or your hoodie, and put a dress on. Put on tight pants with heels. Stilettos will not only lift your height, they will also lift your spirits. Try it. You could be in the crappiest mood and be so tired, but something about walking in high heels—maybe it's having to keep balanced or keep your back perfectly aligned the whole time—makes you walk taller and feel taller. It commands attention in that positive way I mentioned, rather than you getting attention for being sulky and depressed looking. Iron a shirt and put on a fancy bra. You may still feel like utter shit on the inside, but at least you're putting on an air of, "Hey, I got this. I'm okay."

Don't forget to shave your legs, which perhaps hasn't been done since the last time you saw your ex. We must get back to the pristine personal hygiene that we used to value. The bikini waxes, getting your brows done, getting rid of any facial hair for that matter, the floral liquid soaps in your shower, the biweekly manicures and pedicures—get back into the routine of turning yourself into a shiny penny again. Your glow will radiate outward. Put in the effort and make it happen.

Before you go to that party or dinner, make a stop at your local cosmetics counter and get your makeup professionally done. There's something about showing up somewhere looking like you are on top of the world even if you don't really feel like it. Flawless makeup will make you smile. Do pretty and the rest will follow.

Now for the body. A deep tissue massage will release all the stress you've been storing. It won't magically disappear, but during that time on the table, someone will be easing a bit of your physical pain. Drink plenty of water afterward to flush it all out of your system. You will stand a bit taller the next day. While you're at the spa, get a facial. Stress and anxiety cause breakouts and make your skin look older than you probably are, so having an esthetician work their magic on your face will feel incredible *and* you'll leave looking like a million bucks. While you're there, don't skip the sauna or that special quiet room some spas have. Just be still and let people take care of you.

Then there's the car. Post-split, when I finally brought my SUV into the car wash to get the works done, after my black vehicle had this grayish hue going on for a while, I felt like I was metaphorically washing away some of my past and moving on to a bright, clean future. Driving around in a shined-up car brought me a sense of calm and purpose, something a bottle of wine didn't really do. I suggest spending some extra cash on getting your car detailed, too. You know that car wash option you never get because it's too expensive, because a clean car is a clean car? Do it. Getting your car detailed is special. Do it once, at least. You will feel better about yourself behind the wheel, which will make a difference when you step out of your car, too.

Then there's the house cleanup. Get rid of the clutter. And if there's one thing in your home that will help you feel like you can conquer the world while you're sad, besides maybe your coffee maker, it is a clean, made bed. I may sound like your mother right now, but after you wake up in the morning, make your bed. Have it be the first thing you do in the morning, even before you go to the bathroom, because the minute you move away from the bed and start your morning routine, making the bed becomes your last priority, and then it never gets done. Then the whole week has gone by and the bed has become a wrinkled, disheveled mess. Sort of like you feel right about now, huh? There is just something about a crisp, well-made bed with all the pillows neatly organized that will help put you on a neatly organized and balanced day. I haven't even mentioned what clean sheets do for the soul. There is no feeling quite like slipping into a bed with freshly laundered bedding. With a calm, neat, and serene bed, somehow life doesn't seem quite as chaotic.

If you have spare cash, having a professional clean your place can do wonders for your well-being. To this day, I have an amazing housekeeper who comes to my house every two weeks and makes it sparkle. I am so grateful to be able to come home after she's been there to a beautifully clean home. That always makes me feel really good, and my immaculate house becomes one less thing I have to worry about. And that's why we are here, to let go of some of what we are worrying about during an otherwise hard time.

All these housekeeping steps, personal and domestic, *will* really help you feel better about yourself. You are working so hard at healing yourself from the inside; think of this exterior detailing work as rewarding yourself for all that hard work. Inner work is the hardest work of all, but with all these feel-good suggestions, all that work won't show on your face, body, and home so much. I believe L'Oréal said it best: "Because you're worth it."

 YOUR TURN: Make an appointment with your hairdresser. Make an appointment at your local makeup counter. Make an appointment for a deep tissue massage. Drive to your local car wash. Spend the extra cash.

REMEMBER THE RED FLAGS

But we were so good together.
But it was the best chemistry I've ever had.
Only he knows how to do that thing I like.
But his friends love me.
But we went on that trip one time and he said those words to me.
Maybe he's just scared right now.
But I know how he really feels.
But, but, but . . .

After you experience a loss like this, you may find yourself remembering only the good times. All the fun you had together, all the meals you made together, all the restaurants you went to together, all the vacations you took together, the ridiculous, epic chemistry the two of you had that can never be replaced, all the baby names you picked out for your children. You get the idea. I know you miss your man. I missed my man every day. When your heart is broken and you're the loneliest you've ever been, your mind will automatically revert to all the days, months, and years of good and wonderful memories. It's totally natural. But let me stop you right there and wake you up from your delusional coma. You guys broke up for a reason, and that reason has probably been banging on your door for quite some time now.

I define a red flag as something you know in your heart is not supposed to be happening, but you allow to happen anyway. Or something your boyfriend does that makes your heart and stomach ache, but you do nothing and say nothing until it's too late. I would venture a guess that you might know what a red flag is and probably had many of them in your previous relationship. Lying. Cheating. Withholding information. Abuse of any kind, verbal or physical. The list could go from small warning signs to quite obvious, in-your-face signs that scream out that you need to stay away. Within my little bubble, the universe was trying to communicate something to me, whether I was aware of it or not, but I chose to ignore all the signs. Here are some of mine.

Mr. My Big still communicating *and hanging out with* Natasha while we were together. Something I tolerated even though I knew in my heart it was not the right thing to do. The notion of "staying friends with the ex" *is* a topic debated about often, and I don't think there is a strict rule on the matter. I have dated guys, great guys, who are still friends with their exes and it's never been a problem. Just be sure you have all the facts. Even then, if you can't decipher the lies from the truth, you'll have to go with your gut. The blatant back-and-forth Mr. My Big did between Natasha and me is quite possibly the biggest red flag. But then again, him telling me he got an engagement ring, even though he was saying he wasn't sure he was going to give it to her, is a big red flag, and should have sent me running the other way.

More red flags: Mr. My Big liked to flirt with other women. If I ever mentioned it he'd say it was nothing. I didn't know what to believe, given his history. Guys in general sometimes do flirt, whether or not they are in a relationship or even if they're married. Again, just be sure if it's harmless fun or if it's something you should be worrying about. Listen, I'm not a saint either. I flirt in certain scenarios. I'm just saying if your man's behavior is making your stomach flip, pay attention to that feeling.

Another one: He never really told any of his friends how serious we really were. When certain groups of friends got together, we'd either not go at all or he'd go without me. I hated when the latter happened, and I fought it all the time. We never went on double dates with a certain group of his friends, and I asked about doing that all the time. Regardless of the reason that would happen, so that Natasha wouldn't find out about us or the shame around our relationship, it still hurt. Mr. My Big would cancel some of our trips at the last minute for various reasons, none of which I thought were worthy excuses. I stayed mad and broke up with him a few times over it, but he always came back in some fashion or another, and I always took him back. It was a sad, never-ending cycle. Let me tell you how amazing it feels to have woken up from that red flag–plagued drama. I am a whole new person now, and you can be too, just get your head out of your ass and see what's going on.

Every time my mind went to the nicknames we had for each other, the cuddling, the sushi takeout we ate, the stray cat we took in as our own, the sports teams we rooted for together, the love we had for each other—I *always* went to the red flag folder in my mind. It's that place in my head where I stored all the horrible, mean, unimaginable things Mr. My Big was capable of and that I put up with. Of course, there were times when I would get really sad and angry about what had occurred, but after much soul-searching, I realized I was sad and angry with *myself* for allowing it to go on as long as it did. I made all those choices, and I made the decision each and every time to go back to him. My moments of insanity and *wanting* to leave him for every red flag quickly turned into passionate makeup sessions that I couldn't say no to. But why would I want to be with a person like that? That thought set me back in the right place, each and every time.

Mr. My Big also didn't say, "I love you." He only said it after we broke up. To this hopeless romantic, "I love you" is non-negotiable. Well, now it's non-negotiable. But it's not like I was only waiting for him to say it to me. I did tell him I loved him, and then we'd have the same conversation afterward—that a piece of his heart was elsewhere and until he fully had it back, he couldn't give it to someone else. Natasha haunted our existence, probably just as much as I haunted hers. If she only knew. "Lesley, get out of there," I wish I could say to myself. But no, I stayed and had that same discussion with him over and over again. It's kind of like continually getting hit with a two-by-four on your head but not getting out of the hitter's way. They say love is blind. Yeah, love is blind, deaf, and dumb sometimes. It's also often delusional, stubborn, and slightly pathetic. Red flags, ladies. Red flags.

While Mr. My Big was on his journey to work out whatever he needed to work out, when our time together was over, I had to pick up the pieces and carry on with my life without him. And by consciously choosing what my thoughts were, I could choose to remember the red flags instead of harping on what I missed about him. It helped me see why I was not meant to be in that relationship. I mean, seriously, crazy behavior drove me crazy. And I couldn't live like that.

Every relationship is different, and no one knows what goes on behind closed doors between two people, so I can't tell you what red flags you had going on in your relationship. But many of them are universal. Sometimes, if you communicate your feelings about any red flags you are noticing, things will improve between you two. *But*, since this is a book about how to survive a broken heart and not how to save your relationship, the red flags you felt *were* there to stay and there was nothing you could have done about them. Listen to your gut on this one. Really listen. It will never steer you wrong.

 YOUR TURN: Since remembering the good moments is easy and won't help you much at this time, I want you to write down all the red flags you noticed in your past relationship. All of them. Don't be shy. You need honesty in order to heal and find healthy love in your life.

BE PATIENT

Now, after your breakup, is the time you need to chill more than ever. Find your strength and your confidence and take a step back from the situation. Just stop all the madness, go live your life, and watch what happens.

The problem with achieving this is that modern life is more and more about instant gratification. I'm guilty of constantly checking my Twitter feed for the latest breaking news or to see what's happening in the world. Information gets communicated within seconds. The conflict with such a standard is that speed does not pertain to our personal lives, in dating and especially in healing. Healing is in no way instant, and you will not get gratification until way down the road. Try to speed up the process, skip steps, or, as I like to call it, Band-Aid your emotional bruises, and you'll lose. Your grief will be waiting for you next time around. Don't rush the process. I promise it gets better.

I really didn't want to put this cliché in my book, but I have to because it's the truth: Time heals all wounds. And I am not repeating this over-used and slightly annoying quote to make you feel better. I'm saying it because it's true. You won't realize time is passing while you are on the floor crying, or when you can't get out of bed for days, but a few weeks down the road, maybe months, you will notice that you feel a little bit better than you did when the bomb was dropped. I know you don't feel that way right now, but I want you to just trust me on this.

The heart is a muscle that will pull, tear, ache, bruise, be sore, and get injured. And when the heart gets hurt, like muscles often do, it too will need time to heal. You know when you pull a muscle in your back and your physical therapist tells you not to work out for four weeks because the muscle needs to time to heal? You know when you pull a muscle in your leg and you can't run every day like you want to because you need to let it heal? How about that time you woke up to find you somehow slept wrong and all the muscles in your neck were stiff, and you had to ease up on the gym and sleep in a different position until the muscles didn't ache anymore? You know when you've hurt a muscle so badly you need to go see a doctor or specialist who knows how to delicately treat said muscle in order to heal it properly? Giving these muscles time, and perhaps the proper person to heal them, is what you always do, so why should your *heart* be any different? That, too, is a muscle.

When I asked my friend Kimberly to describe what a breakup is like for her, she said, "Breaking up is like getting together. Both take time." There's that word again. Time. Letting go of *anything* is frickin' hard, so letting go of another human being you've invested time and energy is beyond tough. Cut yourself some slack, girl. Take the time to heal. No one expects you to be your rosy, cheerful self tomorrow, so don't worry about it. And speaking of worrying. Worrying about what will be in the future is a waste of your time. You have just as much control of what's going to happen in the future as you did the breakup you are currently going through.

Instead, try the opposite of worry, which is being grateful, knowing and accepting you are in the very place you are meant to be at this given time and being thankful for all you have in that moment. It's the higher power, or whatever you want to call it, that always seems to make things right in the end. When you continually are trying for something and it's just not working, and then you take a step back for a minute and leave it alone, the universe sort of smooths out the edges a bit and puts the puzzle back together in the way you never imagined. You may not have envisioned the picture this puzzle has created, but that's all part of it, too. It all never really comes together the way you think, hope, or plan, but it somehow all works out for the best.

When will you be back to normal? I don't think you ever go back to the way you were before a breakup, and to be honest, I wouldn't want to go back to who *I* was at that time. I officially got over the grief-hump when Mr. My Big married Natasha. He was getting married in the same town we both lived, so I booked a trip to go back east that weekend. I couldn't conceive of being in town while he was getting married. That weekend was still tough to get through, even three thousand miles away, but something miraculous happened when I got back to LA. It didn't hurt anymore. I felt like a massive weight had been lifted off my shoulders the day after their wedding. I thought I would be more upset after he got married, but I actually felt the biggest release of my life. That's all it took. Seriously God, you couldn't take him off the market sooner? Of course He couldn't, because that would mean I wouldn't have gone through all the hardships, lessons, and personal growth that comes with the process. You too will have that moment. Just hold on.

Sometimes all you can do is not think, not wonder, not imagine, and not obsess. Just breathe, in this very minute, and have faith that everything will work out for the best. I have no idea who told me this quote, but I've been saying it forever. "You want to hear God laugh, tell him your plan." God, or whatever you believe in, always has the final say in things, so you might as well accept that now. You are not in control.

One of my favorite books is *The Count of Monte Cristo* by Alexandre Dumas, the ultimate story of survival, patience, and revenge. While the entire classic is filled with brilliant one-liners, my favorite is the last line. "'My dear,' replied Valentine, 'has not the Count just told us that all human wisdom is contained in the words, 'Wait and hope!''"

Wait and hope. Man, it gets me every time.

Now you may be thinking, will the universe put another good-looking and interesting guy in front of me ever again? You're probably obsessing every second of the day that you are going to wind up being alone for the rest of your life. But then something happens. I don't know when, how, or why, but something happens. You are just being you. You feel pretty good. You're pretty sure you look good too, but you're really itching for a connection of some kind. Something. Someone. You become curious again. Your eyes scan the scene, seeking out a bond. That *je ne sais quoi*. You take it all in. You're out, what the hell else are you going do? Nothing is really grabbing you. *He's not cute. No way would I want to be with that guy. Yeah, he's not the one. Nope, not him either. No way. Ugh, why am I out right now when I could be home in my sweats watching the Food Network. This sucks.*

Wait. And then... and then... and then your eyes meet. *What was that? Is that real? Oh yeah, there's definitely something there. What is that something? What is it? There's an energy in the air. Is that chemical? Biological? Hormonal? What is it?* You want to reach out and touch him. You think you should be touching him. Kissing him, perhaps? *I think he likes me. What happens now? Who's going to say something first? Will he? Should I? Oh my God, he's looking over. Should I make eye contact? I want him to know I'm interested in him, but does that mean I should maintain eye contact or look away and play coy? If I play coy and he walks away, I will have wished I said something and not played coy. But if I say something rather than play coy and he blows me off, then I'll feel really stupid and wished I played coy.*

The decision-making process you're forced to engage in right now is driving you slightly insane. *Why is this so hard? Isn't this supposed to be easy, effortless, natural? Isn't the guy automatically supposed to make the first move? Why am I even thinking about saying something? He's the man, for goodness sake. It's his role in life to be the hunter, the seeker, the first mover.* You don't want to have to play the role of the aggressor. *No.* You won't do it. If he wants to talk to you, he has to make the first move. *That's it. Yes.* You've made up your mind. That's how it should be. You're a lady. If he wants you he'll come and get you. *But wait, what happens if he really is interested but gets scared and doesn't make the first move, then will all of this flirting be for nothing?*

Oh my God, he's coming over here. What do I do? Should I say something? Is he gonna say something? Oh my God, Oh my God, Oh my... "Oh, hey. How's it going?" Sigh.

Told you.

 YOUR TURN: Keep reading this book and follow my suggestions on surviving and healing a broken heart. Time will pass while you are doing it all . . . and in the not-so-distant future you'll learn why this chapter is undeniable.

LISTEN AND LEARN

Lesley has the biggest heart of anyone I know. She is an extremely passionate, loving, and caring person. She believes in love at first sight, The One, and everything a hopeless romantic believes in.

Note, SHE AND I ARE TOTALLY OPPOSITE . . . so not sure I am worthy of writing this.

Lesley gave everything she had to the relationship she was in, 200 percent and then some. The problem was, she was giving to the wrong person. He was not deserving of her love. Nonetheless, that is the type of person she is . . . she gives and gives, and loves and loves, no matter what. That is what is so exceptional about her.

The breakup was extremely difficult. Excruciating may be a better choice of words. When most people would have walked away a long time ago . . . given her character, she stayed in it. However, staying in it made the pain and heartbreak even more agonizing. It was a very sad time to see her hurt so much. Nothing I could say or

do could make it better. If only she could see that he wasn't worth
her tears. But she had to feel and experience the breakup for herself
and learn that she would be better without him. She was on a
long, dark road for some time and then something clicked. Just like
that, she was on a new road . . . a new path. I am not sure what it
was . . . maybe she realized that she deserved more.

And I am so happy that the fun-loving Lesley is back. She has
returned from the deep haunting of Mr. X.
Xoxo,
The BFF

Putting this book together a couple years after the first breakup
went down, I started to question if indeed my broken heart
was as horrible as I had remembered. I asked a few women in
my life to tell me what they experienced from the outside looking in
on my relationship and me over those years so I could gain a bit more
clarity on the matter. It's amazing to hear their words after the fact. I
am now able to fully understand what they had to put up with. I love
them even more.

One of the friends is Andrea, the girl I went to Atlanta with. She's
the wise one who threatened to post that sad picture of me on Facebook.
I was at her house one day, and I decided to sit down with her to really
listen to what my breakup sounded like from another perspective. And
I decided to record it. This chapter is near the end of the book because
earlier in your breakup, you are not going to want to listen to anyone
tell you what they think of you and your situation. And even if you do
listen, it's not going to be anything you want to hear, nor is it advice you
are likely to take. Let's be honest with ourselves. Most people I know
have to experience something to really learn the lessons.

Here I was, sitting in sweats on a balcony in the Hollywood Hills
one Sunday morning, drinking coffee with one of the few women in my

life who knows me almost as well as I know myself. If I ever need a good dose of tough love, this is the girl I talk to. I taped our conversation, transcribed it, and am including a lot of it here. Our talk was about an hour and a half long, so obviously I'm not including the entire conversation, but trust me, I didn't leave out anything that should be in this chapter.

ME: So as I'm writing, going into all this crap, actually having to talk about it again, I'm thinking, there's no way it could of been that bad. There's no way I could have been that depressed that I can't see my friends, my best friends who have been there through everything. It could not have been that bad that I checked out of life. It couldn't have been as bad as . . .

ANDREA: That's what we all thought, like, what the hell's wrong with you? You know when something incredibly traumatic happens and then you don't want to relive that feeling, so you're like, it wasn't that bad. It couldn't have been that bad where you're like you can't allow yourself to even feel that anymore or even remember what that feeling is. Something in your body blocks it out because it was trauma. So you can't process it emotionally anymore, like the thought actually doesn't even click into place. It's your body's way of protecting itself. Your body does something to keep you from feeling that feeling again. So it could be a reason why you're sitting here saying, it wasn't that bad. It's your body's way of coping with pain. It's not reality. It was bad. It doesn't just suddenly disappear.

ME: That doesn't mean it's not healed, because I'm healed.

ANDREA: Well, yeah. It just means the thought and the ability or idea to bring it up again, to process it in a way is like, you can't actually feel those things again or really go into what it felt like. It's like when someone dies, when someone tells the story of someone dying a few years later, the emotions aren't attached to the story, they're just not, and the person has healed from the person's death. But that doesn't mean that the ability to explain what you were going through at the time is difficult once time has been put between the two things. And you can maybe talk about it, but, while you're saying it couldn't of been that bad, you can have the conversation, but I think attaching the feeling to what you were going through at the time is probably hard at this point to piece together.

ME: I now can say the whole situation was all about me and it had nothing to do with him. So, as the person who saw all of it from day one, on and off . . .

ANDREA: I mean, I saw a lot of . . . you had an enormous amount of angst on a daily basis, which was making you emotionally not in control and doing things that were borderline psychotic for the sake of love but it had gotten to a point where it was so far beyond trying to make a relationship work. Which is what I don't understand, and not just you, it's a lot of women. The lengths that some women go to, to get the man, it's almost like, is it getting the *man* or is it *getting* the man. You know what I mean? What's the difference? You wanted him to get caught. You were hoping something would happen with the two of you so she would go away, so you could have him, but why would you want that?

ME: Now I can see that.

ANDREA: Yeah, I mean that's the question. It's like women who stay with abusers or stay with cheaters. It's like, what are you fighting for exactly? I'm totally confused. What is that? Why would you ever want to fight for someone who is a horrible person? Who is horrible, not to you necessarily, but just as far as morals and values and integrity in their life. I think that was what our argument was all the time with you, but then why would you want to be with him when he's doing this to her? When he's cheating on her with you, you think that at some point, it's not gonna happen to you, you're sorely mistaken, cause it's going to. And it will happen to another person he's with. It's going to. It's just the way he is. Anyone who can do that and still put a ring on her finger, it's disgusting. It's true. I mean, that's horrible, and what's worse is that she knows somewhere. She's a woman. We all know. You knew what was going on . . .

ME: Well, she met me a few different times.

ANDREA: You knew, I'm sure there was a large part of you that went, which is what sent you into panic mode, "Oh my God, he's actually, he's not gonna be with me. Oh my God, I'm gonna lose," which probably made you fight even harder. There had to be a larger part of you that knew that, that panicked, and knew that you weren't gonna be the one to get the ring. Even though you couldn't understand it and you only heard his side of the story, you knew there was something in that relationship that kept him in it. It was just a sick, twisted game of manipulation. And I think as your friends on the outside to see this pretty clever game that he was able to pull off, which is fascinating, I mean, it's crazy.

ME: I really loved him but sometimes I used to think they could make *Dateline* specials about him.

ANDREA: Yeah, it's nuts! They do. They're on every Saturday. I just watched one the other day about a man who had seven wives and none of them knew about each other. How? Where's your husband going for four nights out of the week when he's with the other women? How? People fucking do it. Are you kidding? I have no idea. I don't know how it happens. Women just turn a blind eye. I think if he ever gave you one hundred percent that you'd probably be over it. I think what kept you excited and around and intrigued was the intrigue because you never got him one hundred percent. Even when you were in your relationship, when he was with just you, you didn't know if he was seeing N—— at all, you didn't know if he was going to P—— to see N——, you didn't know if he was going to M—— and then he decided to not take you. He always left like fifteen percent of himself out of your relationship, which is what actually kept you there as long as you were. I think if he was one hundred percent, then you'd be like, ehhh. Okay, I have it. It's not really what I thought it was. It kept you from having to look at yourself because you spent so much time thinking about what he was doing and focusing on him that for all those years you didn't have to worry about yourself. Which is devastating for your friends to watch, because we knew the crazy web that he was weaving and you were right in it and you couldn't even see it. And it's good that she finally found out, but it's like, who cares if she knew. It was about you knowing what he was doing and you should have been the one to leave.

ME: I wasn't strong enough.

ANDREA: Not even getting involved in that. Obviously you're not gonna waste any more time. It's hard to feel empathy and support for your friends when all you want to do is get angry at them because you can only hold somebody, talk to somebody, and love someone when they're going through something. You know, touch hot stove once, touch it again you're going to get smacked. So it's like, didn't you learn? You know the outcome of this, so what are you doing? Why would you put yourself through that?

ME: This is so eye-opening because I thought you'd say, oh you were so sad, you were . . .

ANDREA: You were maniacal. You weren't sad. You were, like, in a crazy place. I would say for three years. Then you were good for a minute and then he shows back up again. But shows up again with a ring in his pocket for somebody else . . . to tell you about it after he flirts. I was never there for what you guys had behind closed doors. It seems, like you said, *Dateline* special. What's the motivation there other than to completely destroy you? To come back for one more kick in the face. You were already down. You were trying to pick yourself back up. He kept kicking you and you were holding on to the fact that he wasn't gonna give her the ring, he would of married you . . . but you would have married someone that was kicking you in the face when you're down? That's what was happening with all your friends, we were all going, I don't understand it. You're this great, strong, beautiful, intelligent woman who's got her shit banging . . . and with this relationship in particular, it had gone above and beyond. It wasn't healthy from the moment you started dating him because he still had a relationship with his ex. Maybe not physically, but emotionally is worse. From the moment you guys first started.

ME: The whole relationship, he didn't say, "I love you." Then after he breaks up with me, the following year running into him, then he says, "I love you." *Now* it's, I love you? He came back, had a ring for her and an "I love you" for me. An "I love you" for me is—you don't throw that around.

ANDREA: Sick. It was manipulative.

ME: I wasn't strong enough to walk away, but I was getting there.

ANDREA: What I think you need to relate to women, and what I've tried to over the years is, like you've said, you all wait for the guy to stop calling and stop coming around and leading you on for you to leave. It's not their responsibility. Why would they? They have no reason to. When they call, when they come around, when they come over, you flirt, you give them the attention they want . . . so why would they stop coming around? You give them everything they want. They give you nothing. So what would be their reason other than to respect your wishes, which they never have from the beginning?

ME: You think even the good guys?

ANDREA: Good guys don't do that. We're talking about a cheater or someone who is a fucking manipulator. That particular man doesn't care about anyone else but himself. They want just what feels good. They want the attention. Don't open the door. We lock our doors at night cause we don't want that in. We protect ourselves. Don't open the door. You don't make excuses. A man is very simple. They tell you who they are from the very beginning. Women don't listen. How many times can a man say, "I'm not ready"? And a woman goes, "I'll make him ready. He'll change his mind." Um, actually, you're not going to. Not gonna happen. It never happens. And if they do, it's because they've been pressured and they're tired of hearing you nag and they're gonna resent you for the rest of your relationship, which is gonna be short lived.

ME: You know what I just thought of, and this goes the complete other way, it's almost as if women break their own hearts.

ANDREA: They do. The men that break our hearts are men that we allow in our lives that we know are gonna hurt us, because when you allow yourself to fall in love with a man that deserves it, you both do everything you can to make it work, together as a team. And when you get hurt, it's because you've allowed yourself to be vulnerable with someone that doesn't get it, that's gonna shit on you. That's the million-dollar question, why don't some women realize their worth? I don't know, your friends were sitting around going, I cannot believe that you're still there. I cannot believe you're still allowing yourself to still be upset, to be angry, to be in pain. Every day it was affecting your work. You were torturing yourself. It's like you had it over and over and over again and you still ignored it and stayed in the situation. Shame on him. Shame on him. It's just so awful of a person. Like, that's not okay. Its sucks that women have to see it to believe it, even though there's writing all over the wall. And then you see it and then you still stay. It's like, what was it gonna take? If he would just stop calling? If he would just go away? No, don't answer your phone.

ME: It took hitting rock bottom to get the strength.

ANDREA: But you did, and now you see it, and now you're out of the storm and you're able to look at other people going through it and go, I cannot believe I was like that. I cannot believe it. And now you want to tell them, "Oh, if you just find the strength to let it go, you're gonna get everything you want in life. You don't even know it, but I promise you it will happen. When you find the strength to let go you'll get what you want in life, I promise it'll happen. You don't need to settle." And women don't believe it. There are so many women in that, and you can turn around and say, "I did it." I say to them, trust that you are good enough. Stop trying to convince them. Stop. All you have to do is just be. It's just easy.

ME: The guy has to be ready to marry you though. It's timing.

ANDREA: Yes, they have to be ready. It is timing. It's about confidence and security and just owning it.

ME: And women need not be fearful to have that conversation because it's what you want and need.

ANDREA: Yeah, it's okay to say to someone, "This is what I want. This is what I need. In a relationship, I require this. I need this. Can you give this to me?" And listen to what they say, and when they answer you and your gut goes "Eeehhhhh, I don't like that answer," leave. Don't forget that feeling. You knew he was lying so you should have bolted. That's it. It's about knowing what you want and not settling for less. When there's nothing, don't look for something. But when your gut goes off, pay attention to that feeling.

ME: You listen! If I take away anything from sitting down with you, I've known you for a bazillion years, you listen every second I talk!

ANDREA: Of course! I get it. Which is why you made me crazy all the years with M—— because you weren't listening to yourself. I was hearing all of it over and over and over and over again but the story was the same. That's why I'm like, I'm gonna kill this girl. She is not listening to herself. But I was hearing all of it.

ME: You listen! I love you.

 YOUR TURN: After you feel a better and you're more healed than suffering, sit down with a good friend and let them talk about what you were like from their point of view.

HAVE GRATITUDE

You must choose happiness. Choose happiness and be grateful. Stop grieving the loss of this guy for a minute, and simply have gratitude for all that you do have right now in front of you. I promise that process alone will help you move forward. You'll slowly start seeing life beyond the breakup, and eventually life won't be about the breakup at all.

Happiness is a choice, not a place you get to. It's a way of being, not a destination. The people you see running around the world with smiles on their faces, enjoying life, do not necessarily have better lives than you, nor is everything in their lives perfect. They could be going through a breakup just like you. What's going on with them is they are probably choosing to be happy, and that is the only way. When things *aren't* going your way, like during this breakup, you must fight for your own happiness. If you keep looking on the outside for validation, especially from a man, you will lose. I'm not saying going to a beautiful island won't make you happy or winning the lottery won't make your life a bit easier, but the happiness you'll experience from those things will be fleeting. It must come from within. Choose happiness. Not for anyone else, but for yourself.

I totally understand that after a man leaves the last thing you may want to do is smell the roses. I get it. But while your heart is broken and you can't seem to get up off the floor, there are already ready-made happy things in the world waiting for you to just acknowledge them. It's not like you have to reinvent the happy wheel to see things that inspire happiness. There really is so much at your fingertips to help you get through the day. A smile, a laugh, or a warm feeling may not happen right away, but everywhere in life there are the little things to remind us that it's okay to smile, it's okay to be happy, even if you are the saddest you have ever been. There are things in life that will always make you smile.

What little things in life make you happy? Write them down. To help you start your list, I will offer an excerpt from mine. This is a list I actually started about ten years ago, after seeing another author do the same thing and write a book about it. The book is called *14,000 Things to be Happy About* and is by Barbara Ann Kipfer. This book still sits on my bookshelf. Inspired, I started my own list just for kicks. The list grew and grew slowly over the years, and wherever I went I was always jotting things down to add to my collection. Just the act of writing some of these things down put a smile on my face.

This is an excerpt from my full list. See the complete list in the appendix. These happy things are something you can revisit at any time.

1. The smell of Tide
2. Coffee in the morning, afternoon, and night
3. Hitting the exact dollar when pumping gas
4. Waking up without an alarm clock

5. Hot chicken noodle soup on a chilly day
6. Mom and Dad
7. Listening to someone playing the piano
8. Talking to dogs you pass on the street
9. 1950s anything
10. Going out for brunch with your friends on the weekend
11. Lying in bed reading
12. Doing anything in bed
13. Crunchy almond butter on brown rice cakes
14. When he texts you first
15. A complete stranger helping you with your luggage
16. Looking at old black-and-white photos of your parents and grandparents
17. Netflix
18. Mechanical pencils
19. New black clothing
20. Spooning and you're the little spoon
21. Ray-Ban aviator sunglasses
22. Having the shop owners in your neighborhood know you by name
23. Finding a heads-up penny just when you need it
24. The sound of a wine or champagne bottle opening
25. Playing with the animals at the pet store

 YOUR TURN: Throughout your day, write down EVERYTHING that makes you smile or laugh.

MY HAPPY ENDING CAN BE YOURS

Going through a breakup *is* one of the worst experiences out there. If you had told me during that time I'd come out of that mess a stronger and wiser person, I would have thought you were crazy. Remember, no matter how bad things are, no matter how heartbroken you feel, you will survive and live to talk about, probably even laugh about it. Or, like me, write about it.

I heard someone say once that when you dig into the what-went-wrongs and the who-did-whats, sometimes you wind up just plain dirty. But here, dirty is good. What I've figured out along the way is that if you ignore what you went through in your relationship and during your breakup, you won't have learned a damn thing and won't become a better person for it. You won't have retained any lessons. You won't put a stop to your destructive behaviors that put you in your unhealthy relationship to begin with. Self-reflection *is* actually the only thing you should be focusing on right now, because you want to have a better knowledge of where you've been and where you are going.

The "we break our own hearts" idea I thought of during my conversation with Andrea stayed on my mind for a while after that talk, and never left. Women really do break their own hearts. We do. I feel like, by staying in a relationship when we know in our hearts it's not for us, or the other person isn't treating us the way we should be treated, or we actually do believe there is someone else better suited out there for us, we are breaking our own hearts and setting ourselves up for failure. Why do some women do that to themselves? Is it fear of being alone? Is it perhaps all about comfort and security over real love?

Let's take someone staying in a job they can't stand. You hear it all the time, how someone doesn't like their job anymore, they're not being treated fairly, there isn't any growth happening, they feel stuck. Yet they stay in that exact position for a variety of reasons, be it money, safety, security, lack of motivation to move on, you name it. I can't say I know what goes on inside another person's head if someone settles into a career they don't feel passionate about. But maybe that's what separates certain people from other people, one has an incurable passionate side that won't ever stop seeking growth and movement while the other wants to remain as is.

I knew my relationship was failing. Yet, as if I was aboard a sinking ship, instead of jumping off the doomed vessel before it went completely under, being able to jump on a life boat, and only suffering a little before being rescued, I chose to hold onto the sinking ship for dear life as it descended into the dark, deep abyss, until it hit the bottom of the ocean. Then, not only did my boat, my foundation, my relationship, sink, but I was at the bottom of the ocean, unable to breathe. Yet I was still alive, and I had to make my way all the way back to the surface for air. It was a long way down and an even longer way back up.

Why did I choose that path instead of the other one? Why did I stay on the sinking ship, knowing in my heart it was doomed? Knowing in my heart Mr. My Big had feelings for Natasha and I at the same time? Life *is* all about choices, and I'm convinced at this point that hope played a massive part. I was always hoping he would change. Or change his mind. Never, ever think you can change someone. I knew, after our breakup, I wanted to heal and to love and to be loved by someone who deserved it. My hope should have been focused on making *that* happen because *that* hope would never have died. But that's the catch—there is no *should have been*. You can't change the past. It was what it was, and we learn and grow from our experiences so next time we're better equipped to make self-honoring choices.

There are lessons and blessings in every challenge. Sure, my breakup could have ultimately been my undoing. But I wasn't going to let that happen. As tragic as I believed my situation to be, I can now say the breakup was actually—yes—a gift, because I never would have evolved into who I am today otherwise. I wouldn't trade in my newfound strength for the world. I am strong now. I am empowered. I have self-love now.

I've been in many healthy relationships. Even Mr. My Big, the one that broke my heart the hardest, was only doing his best. As was I. It was love, for a time; that I am sure of. You know how I know? Because it changed me, it unglued me, and it made me strive to be the best person I could be. When it was over, I had a choice. I could have continued to be depressed and obsessively complain about what he did to me, or I could have taken the other path—the path I took—and gotten on with things. At a certain point, you have to accept it is over.

The love I had for Mr. My Big had nowhere to go after we broke up, which forced me to put that love into myself and to be the best version of me. Without that self-love, there would have been no growth. Of course, you can love someone and that someone can love you back *even if* you don't have self-love. Anything is possible. But I can almost guarantee that relationship will be ridiculously unhealthy. And then it will hurt even more if, and when, it ends, because deep inside you knew it wasn't right. You knew you weren't really being yourself in that red flag–plagued relationship, and you probably knew in your heart that you two were on borrowed time.

You must own your role in all of it—especially why you wanted to be in *that* specific relationship and why you chose *that* guy. The men we date treat us as we expect to be treated. If your ex treated you poorly, you're putting into the world that behavior is what you will take as acceptable. *Don't* change your ways or your view of yourself after your breakup, and you will attract the same type of man next time. Accepting total responsibility for my part in my dysfunctional relationship and not being a victim through it was a crucial step to moving forward. It's a crucial step in your entire life, not just in a relationship. It took that crisis for me to get off my ass and to change my patterns, cultivate new behaviors, and fight for my stronger self. Ultimately, you will come to figure out the relationship that will need saving is not the one leaving you; it's the one you have with yourself.

I am now witnessing close friends going through the exact same thing I went through in my past relationship and breakup. Their men are telling them they don't want a commitment. Their men are telling them they can't give them what they want. Their men are telling them they can't give them everything they need, and yet these strong, smart, beautiful women keep going back for more. More pain. More suffering. More heartbreak. The worst part, for me, is not being able to do a single thing about it, except to be there when they fall. I see them and I think, that was me just a few years ago. I know what it's like, and I know that whatever anyone said to me about the guy and the situation, I was not going to listen. It's a journey that must be experienced. I truly believe that is the only way for it to be learned. Most often, it will take a drastic occurrence for something to change. And you never really know when it's going to strike. Hopefully, it's figured out sooner rather than later.

I've always believed in living life with no regrets, even after all the years of going back and forth with Mr. My Big. If not for my time with him and what I gained from our relationship, I would never have become the strong and self-loving person I am today. I can now say I am forever grateful for what he contributed to my world, personally and professionally. Yes, these words are really coming from me. I learned so much from him, not only about life, but, of course, about myself. He will be forever in my heart, even though he broke it.

I forgive him. Yes, forgive the guy who hurt you. No matter what you think he did to you, forgive him, because whatever you think he did really has nothing to do with you. It's his stuff. So forgive him. Holding onto that grudge will only keep you miles away from the healing you need. You're not forgiving this person for their benefit, but for your own. You do not want to be tied to that person emotionally for the rest of your life. They hurt you. You've healed. Let it go. Forgive him. Move on.

What I've also learned, even though this one is supposed to be common sense and is a bit cliché, is that three is a crowd. I can't believe I actually put up with something like that for so long. Why would I ever think holding onto a man who I knew in my gut was still emotionally attached to someone else was a wise choice? I think during the difficult times the triangle was going on, somewhere in the back of mind I just believed it would ultimately work out in my favor and I wouldn't have to worry anymore. So I stayed, holding on. I just didn't want to believe the truth of what was going on. I only heard what I wanted to hear. Like Andrea said during our conversation, even if I was the one who got him in the end, why would I want a guy like that? I wouldn't. I can see that now. Again, it's called self-love. Once you have that, the world is yours.

Since the breakup, a saving grace for me has been to remember the old adage: if he cheated on her, he'll cheat on you. I can't say that is always true, but someone, somewhere came up with that saying and people like to throw it around. It's a red flag you can never forget, for your own sake. I'll never know what might have been if I had been the one to wind up with him, because I wasn't given that choice. But would I really have wanted that chance anyway? Would I have grown tired of his antics eventually? I know what that answer is, but knowing the answer doesn't really matter now. I can now see that while I was in it, I never had the strength or the desire to really put my foot down, to send the message that I had had enough. While he was lying to me about so many things, I was, in essence, lying to myself that all was okay. I'd be lying now, too, if I didn't say Mr. My Big *was* the most precious thing in my life for many years.

Every guy you meet isn't going to be The One, and every guy you meet that you want to be with isn't going to want to be with you. It's timing. You could meet the greatest guy in the world, your chemistry could be off the charts, the two of you could share the same passions, hobbies, food interests, taste in movies—but if he is not at the same place you are and he's not ready to settle into the type of relationship you are looking for, it will not work. No matter how much you will it to work, it won't happen. It is all about timing. And love. And trust. Without trust, there is nothing. Love and timing and trust. When you have that combination of things, the stars are aligned and beautiful things happen.

Speaking of finding another partner, I didn't want to tell you this while you were reading the book, because I really wanted you to know where I had been and how hard my breakup was on me, but now I want to tell you where I am now. I am currently in a relationship. A healthy, fun, and exciting relationship. I am seeing someone who is kind, sweet, truthful, witty, ridiculously handsome, and genius smart. I am here to tell you it's out there waiting for you, when you're ready. So go get ready. But while I have shown you a road map for how to navigate through heartbreak, there really isn't a universal road map for finding love. It starts with loving yourself, doing what you love, surrounding yourself with the people who love you and who you love in return, and allowing the universe to take care of the rest. Have faith in *that*.

You cannot persuade someone to love you and you can't make anyone stay. My hope for you is that you never settle for anything less than you deserve. Love, in all its glory and sadness, is a mystery, and no matter how many times you get your heart broken or how many times you fall in love, understanding the opposite sex will not get any easier. You will never, ever know what they are thinking. So stop trying to figure it out and go figure *yourself* out. Just do you, and the rest will follow naturally. That is all you need to understand.

And so begins your own soul-searching. To everyone walking around with the pain from a broken heart, I want you to know it does not last forever. As my parents told me in the very beginning, and still do to this day when I'm facing challenges, there is a light at the end of the tunnel. When you're behind the wheel of your car, you always drive in and then out the other end of a tunnel, don't you? So keep your eyes focused on the road ahead. You can't move forward if you keep looking in the rearview mirror. I read that a long time ago, and it's stayed with me.

This too shall pass. Life will change, your job will change, your acquaintances will change, and your love life will change. Learning not to fight the inevitable changes life brings is a key component to surviving a broken heart. Focus on what you can control and have grace to accept the things you can't. It's the only way you'll get through life. If you keep fighting things out of your control, you will never win. Will you and your ex ever see each other again? Could you and your ex ever get back together? I can't predict the future. My professor also has said about life: "You *never* know." He's right. You never know anything. What I *do* know is all you can focus on is you.

After your breakup, go through life slowly and stay true to what you need in each moment. Wake up, do your thing, and go to bed. Keep doing that. One day, doing your thing becomes doing your things, and another day doing your things becomes doing your things with someone by your side. One day you will wake up, and your ex won't be the first thing you think about. And one day when you go to bed, he won't be the last thing you think about. And one day, when you are warmly wrapped in another man's arms, he won't be what you think about at all. When you go to bed at night, if you really believe you did the best you could that day, that's all you could ask for. Those words of wisdom are something Mr. My Big used to say, and they stuck.

Have hope.

Be optimistic.

Have strength.

Know you will find yourself in a new relationship; you just have to walk the murky, dark path of surviving this breakup before you find yourself there. And if a new relationship with an amazing new man and your amazing new self isn't incentive for surviving your broken heart, then nothing is.

This is the end of the book, but it's really just the beginning. The beginning of the rest of your life.

 YOUR TURN: Live your life.

MY ACCEPTANCE SPEECH

I may not win an Oscar® in my lifetime. Anything is possible, but an Emmy® seems a bit more realistic at this stage considering I have already been nominated for one. Either way, I'm going to use this page to give my acceptance speech. My *acceptance* speech. My acceptance speech to accept and acknowledge where I have been; where I am now; and where I am going. I accept it all. And with an acceptance speech comes the thank yous, which I will never run out of.

As it goes, family is always first. To mom and dad, thank you for always having my back. No matter if the spotlight was shining bright on my head or if there was no light and my stress had gotten the better of me. To my sister, you've put up with me since I was born. I'm thankful for everyday that we talk. I am always listening. And, it seems one thank you to you and my brother-in-law for the two of you creating my munchkin doesn't really do him justice. He is the love of my life.

To the Baker family. You've opened your home and your lives to me, the "third" child, for so long, and I am grateful. To Ken, my mentor and dear friend, thank you for your continued guidance and support.

To my loyal girlfriends. Thank you for loving me through the fantastic times and the heartbreaking ones. You make the journey that much more enjoyable, and to know all of you is to love all of you.

Thank you to The Senator for your wisdom and all the introductions; to my literary agent, Steve Troha at Folio Literary Management, for thinking I had a story to tell; and to Morgan James Publishing for wanting to spread that story to the world.

To USM—love and light.

And I guess things come full circle. Mr. My Big was my muse. That man and his effect on me was the inspiration for this book. For better or for worse. Thank you, Mr. My Big, for our time together. I was there for a reason. Love, yes. Lessons, I'd say so.

ABOUT THE AUTHOR

Lesley Robins is an Emmy® nominated, nationally recognized television and Internet journalist. She is a show producer for *E! News* and an on-air correspondent for *younghollywood.com*. Robins holds a master's degree from the University of Santa Monica in spiritual psychology, a professional designation in journalism with specialization in broadcast from the University of California, Los Angeles, and a bachelor's degree in English and communication from the University of Delaware. She lives in Hermosa Beach, California. You can visit her on Twitter @LesleyMia.

MY HAPPY LIST

1. The smell of Tide
2. Coffee in the morning, afternoon, and night
3. Your first cup of coffee
4. French vanilla creamer
5. Being just out of the shower
6. A big hug
7. Having a conversation with an elderly person
8. Family
9. Talking to your pets
10. Fresh strawberries
11. The perfect banana
12. Another car letting you merge into traffic
13. A new pair of socks
14. Board games

15. Dancing alone in your room
16. Babies
17. Baby Nike shoes
18. School supply shopping
19. Pajamas
20. A bubble bath
21. Hearing your favorite song on the radio
22. Being out of your home state and then seeing a car with your state's license plate
23. Another driver waving to say "thank you" for letting them into traffic
24. A British accent
25. Anything French
26. Hitting the exact dollar when pumping gas
27. Caffeine
28. Getting the Pottery Barn catalog in the mail
29. Photo albums
30. When a stranger stops to compliment you
31. A dog with its head out a moving car's window
32. Flowers
33. Cooking a meal
34. Chocolate
35. Getting a phone call from a person you like
36. Hearing someone say "good job"
37. One of your favorite movies on TV
38. Finishing a book
39. Barbecues
40. Family reunions
41. A phone call from an old friend
42. The perfect bite of food
43. Sleeping late

44. Weekends
45. The moment your plane takes off
46. A glass of wine
47. "Earth Angel" performance in *Back to the Future*
48. Home cooking
49. Buying clothes on sale
50. When you finish exercising
51. Having company at your house
52. Nice salespeople
53. Shakespeare
54. Other happy people
55. Scented candles
56. Pillows and blankets
57. Fuzzy slippers
58. Hot rays of sun on your face
59. Leaving work early
60. A cold can of soda
61. Erasers
62. Cuddling in bed with someone you love
63. Having a clean apartment
64. Getting coupons for the things you use or eat
65. Flannel sheets in the winter
66. Seeing a Broadway show
67. Looking at pictures of you as a baby
68. Opening a present
69. Sleepover parties
70. Ordering in food on a lazy night
71. A lazy night
72. A lazy day
73. Spending the day in your pajamas
74. Doing a good deed

75. Talking to your family on the phone
76. A good cry
77. Getting advice from your parents
78. Accomplishing a goal
79. Finally getting to eat dinner
80. When your parents make everything okay
81. Getting ready for a party
82. Making eye contact with an attractive person
83. Sunshine poking through the clouds
84. The moment you see the baseball field when you go to a stadium
85. Knowing the people you love are well
86. Talking to your grandma
87. A label maker
88. Bowling
89. Diners
90. The wedding section of the *New York Times*
91. Getting real mail from a loved one
92. Good friends
93. A really nice waiter or waitress
94. Making someone else happy
95. Waking up without an alarm clock
96. Meeting someone from your home town
97. Dancing
98. Performing in a show
99. Knowing you were right
100. Chicken soup
101. Clean sheets
102. Opening night
103. Getting flowers
104. Seeing an old flame
105. The instant you get into bed

106. Singing because it feels good
107. Talking to a child
108. Hot soup on a chilly day
109. *Gone with the Wind*
110. Helping someone get a job
111. Painting your toenails
112. Presents
113. Receiving a compliment
114. Watering your plants
115. Cinderella
116. Having a conversation with a three-year-old
117. A long day in comfortable shoes
118. Being in love
119. Dancing at a party
120. Martinis
121. Having an intelligent conversation
122. Respecting someone
123. Flirting
124. Doing anything with your sibling
125. Pictures
126. Reading
127. Seeing your clothes in a magazine
128. Sitting in a law library
129. Feeling really smart
130. Making a new friend
131. Getting a haircut
132. A college campus
133. A warm breeze on a warm night
134. Looking up a word in the dictionary
135. Exploring unfamiliar territory
136. Going home

137. Being a good friend
138. Dreaming
139. Beautiful, sunny mornings
140. Birds chirping
141. House guests
142. Cooking for a dinner party
143. Dancing and sweating
144. Seeing a celebrity you admire
145. Surprising your mom on Mother's Day
146. Being in the home you grew up in
147. Riding a bicycle
148. Lying next to your sister
149. An inside joke
150. When your plane lands
151. Making a new friend
152. Hearing that your best friend got engaged
153. Getting an invitation for your best friend's wedding
154. Being a bridesmaid in your best friend's wedding
155. Shopping
156. Knowing you are going to bed soon
157. Doing absolutely nothing
158. Hiking
159. Breaking the sadness
160. Beach volleyball
161. Driving to the beach with the windows wide open
162. Lying in the sand
163. Getting a tan
164. Collecting seashells on the beach
165. Cooking breakfast
166. Buying a hat
167. Baby stores

168. Being asked out by a boy you like
169. Butterflies in your stomach
170. Going out for dinner
171. Valet parking
172. Villages
173. Flea markets
174. Laughing
175. Falling asleep happy
176. Waking up happy
177. Knowing you look good
178. Baby kittens
179. Getting your developed photos back
180. Learning something new
181. Doing a good deed
182. Celebrating a friend's birthday
183. Making someone happy
184. Trying for something
185. Singing when no one is watching
186. Making dinner with a friend
187. When a friend picks you up at the airport
188. Being a good hostess
189. Believing in yourself
190. Hawai'i
191. When your parents are proud of you
192. Change
193. Slow dancing
194. Good leftovers
195. A stocked refrigerator
196. Getting what you want
197. Airports
198. Airplanes

199. Airplane peanuts
200. Clean teeth after the dentist
201. Kissing
202. Baby talk
203. Waking up in someone's arms
204. When someone says, "I love you"
205. A day at the pool with friends
206. Butter
207. Throwing a BBQ
208. The smell of the air after it rains
209. Friends
210. Listening to others
211. *Sex and the City*
212. Clean towels
213. Spending all day with a friend
214. Taking a walk
215. Buying yourself a present
216. A pet shop
217. Saying goodnight to your pets
218. Wearing your friend's clothes
219. Clear skin
220. Fresh salad with bright-colored vegetables
221. A young, good-looking family
222. People walking their dogs
223. Antique candle holders
224. Talking with a girlfriend all night
225. Being able to call a friend at any time of night
226. Any John Hughes film
227. Watching a classic film
228. Knowing people have your back
229. Receiving a package in the mail

230. Buying a new car
231. Leaving your old car behind
232. New shoes
233. A drink when you need it the most
234. When someone makes you dinner
235. Laughing so hard it hurts to breathe
236. Getting what you want
237. A toasted garlic bagel with warm butter
238. Comfort foods
239. Visiting a historic landmark
240. Feeling rich
241. Looking rich
242. Sweatpants
243. Wearing no underwear
244. College sweatshirts
245. Listening to someone playing the piano
246. Falling in love
247. Getting invited to a party
248. Playing recreational sports
249. Being reminded there are people who care about you
250. Feather blankets and pillows
251. Understanding and appreciating the elderly
252. Holding the door open for someone
253. Nice salespeople
254. Slow dancing
255. Plankton
256. A romantic night on the beach
257. Holding hands with a guy you like
258. Making someone smile and laugh
259. Screaming like no one can hear you
260. The moon and stars

261. Pedicures
262. Manicures
263. Jumping in a pool
264. Sitting in a Jacuzzi
265. Grocery shopping
266. Talking to dogs you pass on the street
267. Sweating
268. Chicken noodle soup with lots of carrots and chicken
269. A cool breeze on a warm night
270. Getting pictures developed
271. Sharpened pencils
272. A new CD (or a new downloaded song off iTunes)
273. Sad movies that make you cry
274. Making business connections
275. Playing Scrabble on an original board
276. Coffee table books
277. Sitting naked in your home
278. Writing in a journal
279. Balconies
280. Mansions
281. A really gorgeous man
282. 1950s anything
283. *The Wizard of Oz*
284. Talking to your ex-boyfriend and realizing you're okay now
285. When a friend realizes she was wrong
286. Making up without a fight
287. Yoga
288. Art collections
289. Tree-lined streets
290. When a waiter forgets to charge you for something
291. Spotting a seal in the ocean

292. Jumping through the waves
293. Playing cards
294. Thinking you are rich
295. Driving through the mountains
296. Not wearing a watch, and not caring what time it is
297. Cheerios with a banana
298. Eating something really fattening and enjoying it
299. A sugar high
300. Getting drunk with your friends and laughing about nothing and everything
301. Business cards with your name on them
302. Finishing a project
303. Being called a rock star
304. Someone buying you a drink
305. A cute bartender
306. Taking off your shoes after a long day
307. Talking with a stranger, yet feeling comfortable
308. Having messages on your voicemail
309. Friday
310. Enjoying your own company
311. Matzo balls
312. Trying a new food dish and really liking it
313. Chenille anything
314. Falling asleep without even trying
315. The bread and butter on the table at an Italian restaurant
316. Mint chocolate chip ice cream
317. Having a crush on someone
318. Kosher delis
319. When an elderly person calls you sweetheart
320. Having a clean house
321. Buying a new pair of jeans

322. Getting invited to a party
323. Hearing that your ex-boyfriend broke up with his current girlfriend
324. Reaching a goal
325. Finding a new goal
326. When your phone rings
327. Getting ready for bed—washing your face and brushing your teeth
328. Going out for breakfast with your friends
329. Answering to no one
330. Knowing you're going to see a person you absolutely adore
331. Playing the White Elephant game at a holiday party
332. Getting a really good deal
333. Sleeping naked
334. Sleeping naked with someone you like
335. Thinking about your wedding
336. Ball gowns
337. Diamonds
338. Love birds
339. Actually enjoying a soap opera
340. That feeling when you're scared, and then you actually go through with it
341. Lying in bed reading
342. Bikini waxes
343. Going on a date with a guy you really like
344. Kissing a boy you really like
345. Sharing food
346. The moment you finish cleaning your bathroom
347. Waking up and seeing a clear blue sky
348. Looking forward to something really exciting
349. *Beverly Hills, 90210* (the TV show)

350. Picking up an old book and rereading the passages you underlined
351. Redecorating your house
352. Buying new lingerie
353. A clean, white tank top
354. Walking by a good-looking guy, and realizing he smells really good, too
355. Tropicana orange juice
356. Cheesecake with whipped cream, chocolate syrup, and strawberries
357. A man singing to you
358. Seeing your friend on TV
359. Spring cleaning
360. Getting your tax rebate in the mail
361. Being asked out on a date
362. Sex
363. Finally getting something done you put off for a long time
364. Your birthday
365. Birthday presents
366. Opening your birthday presents
367. A birthday party
368. People saying, "Happy birthday"
369. The first phone call of the day wishing you a happy birthday
370. Seeing a young family walking down the street
371. Horseback riding
372. Halloween
373. Wearing a costume on Halloween
374. Eating dinner out
375. Seeing your pets happy
376. Knowing the guy you like is thinking about you
377. Sleeping late

378. Jerry Seinfeld
379. Getting a card from your ex-boyfriend
380. Freshly vacuumed carpet
381. Red wine
382. Getting an unexpected, but welcomed wake up call
383. Phone sex
384. Spending a night with friends and playing board games all night
385. Laughing until your stomach muscles hurt
386. Looking for a new job and being optimistic
387. Accomplishing a goal
388. Making vacation plans
389. Clean socks
390. Going to a classy strip club
391. When the boys crash an all-girl slumber party
392. Getting a phone call about a party
393. Short films made by your friends
394. Knowing the words to every 80s song
395. Making eye contact with someone all night and realizing that he felt it, too
396. Coming to terms with how old you are and accepting it
397. Sharing common memories with friends
398. Getting free samples at the grocery store
399. Board games
400. Cute waiters
401. Knowing you can always ask your parents for help
402. Holiday shopping
403. Watching your pets enjoy their food
404. Finally getting to the gym
405. Running scissors through wrapping paper and cutting it in one push
406. Spending the entire day in bed with someone you love

407. Taking a shower with someone you love
408. Sightseeing like you have never done it before
409. Playing at the perfume counter of a department store
410. Kissing forever
411. Getting completely drunk with your friends
412. Kissing a girl just for the heck of it
413. Calling the boy you like for no reason except that you miss him
414. Flannel pajamas
415. The best memories ever
416. A song that makes you feel really good
417. Having pets to make you smile when nothing else will
418. Buying a boyfriend presents
419. Writing in a journal when there is no one to talk to
420. Going to the movies with a friend
421. Listening to new music at the record store
422. Drinking a hot cup of coffee on a cold night
423. Meeting a complete stranger on the street and falling in love
424. Falling in love
425. *Breaking Bad*
426. Knowing you only need one person who understands you
427. Bumping into an old friend
428. Seeing a feel-good movie
429. Watching someone get karma-kicked straight in their ass
430. Crunchy almond butter on brown rice cakes
431. Laughing about yourself
432. Admitting that you are a hopeless romantic and loving every minute of it
433. Knowing in your heart that everything will be okay
434. Fashion bloggers
435. Knowing that you have affected people's lives in this world for the better

436. Christmas music
437. Rockin' to the oldies
438. Dressed warm on a really cold night
439. Broadway tunes
440. That wonderful, untouchable feeling like nothing could ever get any better
441. Being a mentor
442. Having a mentor
443. A dark room with candles burning all around you
444. Looking up airfare in case you decide to fly around the world
445. Getting a text from your crush first
446. Shopping for someone you love
447. Independent movies that have true meaning
448. Reading a newspaper and learning something new
449. When you are exhausted, knowing you are already washed up for bed
450. Seeing old friends
451. Sharing tapas with someone
452. Getting the feeling that everything is going to be all right
453. A perfect steak cooked medium rare with mashed potatoes
454. Always having someone to come home to, even if it is just your pets
455. Getting a check in the mail
456. Watching as your Twitter followers increase
457. House-hunting for no other reason except to look at houses
458. Planning your future when your future is so uncertain
459. Finally going to bed after the longest day in history
460. Having a steamy love affair for a weekend
461. Wrapping a present
462. Taking your makeup off at the end of the day
463. After you move, setting up your new place

464. The friends who help you move
465. Getting a great deal on something you really want
466. A four-post, oak bed with wrought iron trim
467. Filters on Instagram
468. Putting outfits together from your old clothes
469. Going to the doctor to figure out exactly what is wrong
470. Sending out holiday cards
471. Someone cooking you dinner
472. Eating something from your childhood and knowing it tastes so good
473. Hearing that familiar voice that always makes you feel good
474. Lying in bed reading
475. Spending adult time with your parents
476. Having a conversation with your mother about men
477. Planning your wedding down to a tee
478. Mom's homemade chicken noodle soup
479. A brand new apartment with all your old stuff
480. A blanket your grandma knitted
481. Getting a phone call from the person you miss the most
482. Spending two nights in a row with a complete stranger
483. The smell of Sharpie markers
484. A long-awaited kiss
485. Someone calling you talented
486. Knowing that it's going to be okay
487. Having a fling and loving every minute of it
488. The Apple store
489. Gossiping with friends
490. Physical attraction
491. A made bed
492. Television shows that reflect your own life
493. Hearing someone say they need you

494. Spending the holidays with your boyfriend or girlfriend
495. Watering your plants
496. Having professional connections and using them to help other people
497. Allowing fate to take its course
498. Hearing your phone ring and the few seconds before you pick it up, not knowing who it is
499. Getting your home completely remodeled
500. Singing your heart out
501. When your credit card balance is at $0.00
502. "When you realize you want to spend the rest of your life with somebody, you want the rest of your life to start as soon as possible." —Billy Crystal, *When Harry Met Sally*
503. "I'm gonna be a star, 'cause stars don't fall out of the sky." —Lou Diamond Philips, *La Bamba*
504. Planning a vacation
505. Knowing that whatever your mother says is usually right
506. No matter how old you are, always going to your parents first for advice
507. Calling someone to say good morning
508. Walking into a room and seeing a fresh pot of coffee waiting for you
509. Sending greetings cards to your family and friends
510. Loving someone so much that it consumes every cell in your body
511. When someone loves you so much that he moves to your state
512. Realizing that it is time to reinvent yourself, for good
513. Finally understanding that to always go out isn't so important
514. But having the best time ever when you do go out
515. Making a new friend

516. Realizing the friends you've had since the beginning are the keepers
517. Having a secret admirer send you flowers
518. Birds chirping
519. The fresh scent and feel of clean towels
520. Talking to a guy on the phone you have never met, and getting along
521. Making your loved ones smile
522. Calling to apologize when you know you are wrong
523. Free Wi-Fi
524. Spending a romantic weekend with your baby
525. Understanding that everything happens for a reason
526. Love at first sight
527. Not caring what time it is
528. Flirting with someone from across the room
529. Hot soup on a cold night
530. Hot chamomile tea with a little bit of sugar
531. When the wind causes your wind chimes to make music
532. Laughing on the phone with your sibling about absolutely nothing
533. Feeling the sun on your entire body
534. Swimming laps in the pool and just gliding with the water
535. Picking up a hot meal to eat when you are really hungry
536. Flying around the country for love
537. Having a beer all by yourself
538. Sitting on your balcony talking to friend
539. The smell of vanilla
540. Trying on a new bra and knowing you look sexy
541. When he texts you first
542. Not leaving your home all day
543. A clean home

544. Candles lit on a cool night
545. Memories brought up amongst family
546. Sour Patch Kids
547. Staying in bed all day with someone
548. Hot tea before you go to sleep
549. Being utterly surprised
550. The scent of coconut in suntan lotion
551. A complete stranger helping you with your luggage
552. Getting offered a new job
553. Accepting a new job
554. Being inspired by a TV show
555. Friends you can call anytime, anywhere, for any reason
556. Going to Israel
557. Falling in love without even knowing it
558. The time of your life
559. Taking a trip just because
560. Seeing sites you've only read about
561. Baby talk
562. Thanksgiving dinner with family
563. Throwing a party for your friends
564. Having someone to call your boyfriend, and meaning it, and liking it
565. Thinking of a new and original Halloween costume
566. Getting presents during the holidays
567. The anticipation of people opening the gifts that you got them
568. Curling ribbon with a pair of scissors
569. Painting your walls for no other reason than you wanted to
570. Getting free stuff
571. Cooking like you know what you're doing
572. Sharing a bed with your sibling as if you were five years old
573. Watching your plants grow

574. Shrimp scampi with linguini
575. Any piece of art with the word "love" on it
576. Finally reading that article you've been saving for months
577. Lots and lots of kisses
578. Organizing
579. Giving old clothes to Goodwill
580. Feeling comfortable at your boyfriend's parents house
581. Old wrought iron keys
582. A wood-burning fireplace
583. Independence
584. Spontaneity
585. Getting a new recipe and trying it out
586. When the person likes what you've made
587. Paying bills and having the money to do so
588. Doing a good deed
589. House-sitting for a friend
590. The spray from a wave
591. Happy waiters
592. Baskets around your house filled with lots of stuff
593. Hiking with a dog
594. Planning your next vacation
595. Having time to lie down and read a book
596. When the little blue dot under @Connect is lit up on Twitter
597. A clean bathroom floor
598. A clean bathroom
599. Little washcloths at the sinks in fancy hotel bathrooms
600. Getting your photo "liked" on Instagram
601. Unconditional love
602. Eye masks
603. Love letters
604. New, scented candles

605. Going on vacation to visit family
606. Eating hot dogs and hamburgers out on the back porch
607. Seeing wildlife at its best
608. Looking at old black-and-white photos of your parents and grandparents
609. Cleaning out your closet
610. Seeing a celebrity you really admire
611. Getting a workout that kicks your ass
612. A satin robe after a warm bath
613. Meeting a stranger and enjoying your conversation
614. Rearranging the pictures on your wall
615. Walking around a flea market for the entire day
616. Feeling confident in your decisions
617. Having faith that things can only go up
618. Laughing with friends
619. Eating left over birthday cake icing off of the box
620. Coasters
621. Getting a wedding invitation and the envelope is labeled you plus a guest
622. Buying a painting and learning to appreciate it hanging in your house
623. Enjoying the summer for everything it's worth
624. A smiling baby
625. The NYC subway
626. New luggage
627. Making your favorite sandwich
628. Eating your favorite sandwich
629. Not settling for anything less than you want and deserve
630. Witnessing baby birds in their first days of life
631. On the verge of getting a great new job
632. Getting a facial

633. Attending a Fourth of July festival and wearing red, white, and blue
634. Buying brand new white sneakers
635. Buddha
636. Fresh green lettuce
637. Stopping to smell a flower
638. A special magic marker that takes the red out of your eyes in photographs
639. Knowing your parents will never judge you
640. Putting makeup on and feeling pretty
641. Seeing the moon as big as a basketball in your hand
642. Watching the same butterfly come to your garden everyday
643. Knowing that your body is in great shape
644. Making a new best friend
645. Conversations that last for hours and hours
646. Companionship
647. Seeing a loved one you haven't seen in a very long time
648. The Hollywood Bowl
649. The first smell of BBQ
650. Having a beer at that BBQ on a warm, summer day
651. The iPhone
652. Doing nothing in a day with your loved one and having the best day ever
653. Singing Broadway songs in your car at the top of your lungs
654. Getting invited to a party
655. Sitting on your couch eating potato chips and watching TV
656. Roasted butternut squash
657. Setting up your friends on blind dates and hoping they fall in love
658. That one phone call of success

659. The first day when the night becomes chilly and you have to wear a jacket
660. Going to a wedding with your loved one and feeling like a princess
661. Making up with someone close without ever having to say you're sorry
662. A shag carpet
663. Puppies
664. Puppies doing anything
665. Lying on a blanket in the park
666. Warm water hitting your back in the shower
667. Shopping at a vintage fashion flea market
668. Cuddling up on a cold Sunday morning
669. Making soup for yourself
670. Knowing he is in love with you
671. Looking for holiday gifts early
672. Buying a pair of black, high, sexy boots
673. Eating McDonald's and feeling no guilt
674. Having a little extra bounce in your step
675. Having your relatives take you out for dinner when they visit your town
676. Old friends becoming new friends again
677. Holiday bonuses
678. Presents, presents, and more presents
679. Buying a new bikini
680. Christmas caroling
681. Mom and dad
682. Getting rid of all the junk you've been collecting for years
683. Buying new things
684. Roasted vegetables
685. Walking the streets of New York City

686. Taking a chance
687. White linen curtains
688. Free stuff
689. Getting presents after the holiday/birthday has passed
690. "I gotta go see about a girl."—Robin Williams, *Good Will Hunting*
691. Saying "I love you" to your close friends and hearing it back
692. Netflix
693. "I've been dating since I was 16, I'm exhausted, where is he?" —Charlotte, *Sex and the City*
694. A cappella singing
695. Being appreciated at your job
696. When someone laughs at your jokes
697. Courtside seats at a professional basketball game
698. Mechanical pencils
699. Listening to an intelligent person
700. Finding a really good pair of pants that fit
701. Poetic justice
702. Hope
703. The mini red wine bottles on airplanes
704. Manhattan Beach, CA
705. Knowing change is just around the corner
706. "This too shall pass"
707. Confidants
708. Faith
709. A four-year-old's birthday party
710. Understanding the good in having patience
711. Boarding passes on your mobile device
712. Vintage books
713. Brazil
714. The spot on the beach where the ocean meets the sand

715. That moment before your plane touches down
716. Girlfriends
717. When your sister gets engaged
718. Having a stranger say "I love you"
719. New black clothing
720. A chipper barista at Starbucks
721. Sand in a bottle
722. The stamps in your passport
723. Getting a bonus at work
724. When a young child says your name
725. "I guess I just miss my friend." —Morgan Freeman, *Shawshank Redemption*
726. Learning to chill
727. A drama-free day
728. Whole-wheat pita stuffed with turkey, lettuce, and avocado
729. Mangos
730. Lust
731. Spooning in bed—and you're the little spoon
732. *Grey's Anatomy*
733. Playing pool
734. Wearing your guy's sweatshirt that is way too big on you
735. Sleeping in your guy's sweatshirt that is way too big on you
736. Jacuzzis
737. Being pursued for a job you really want
738. Making a new girlfriend
739. Calling an old girlfriend
740. Ray-Ban aviator sunglasses
741. Wish
742. When your pet is up before you
743. The guy you've been in love with for years suddenly becomes available

744. Happy tears
745. Learning how to chill
746. Dance class
747. Prepping for your sister's wedding
748. Therapy
749. Hearing everything you want to hear
750. Crashing boys night
751. Your sister getting married
752. Having options
753. Passion
754. Believing in someone, and them living up to that belief
755. Trust
756. The word "f***"
757. Having the shop owners in your neighborhood know you by name
758. Buying a new car
759. Complimentary coffee at the car wash
760. Being comfortable with your parents paying for gas sometimes
761. Allowing yourself to not always have the answers
762. Getting comfortable with "what is"
763. Sleep
764. Uggs
765. Annual parties
766. Dodger dogs and beer
767. Hip-hop dance class
768. Joel Osteen
769. Eating dinner with your partner at home
770. Cuddling
771. Nicknames
772. Pet names
773. Shower time

774. Taking vacations with your significant other
775. The sound of the coffee maker being done brewing
776. Talking to a stranger while you shop
777. Holiday gift buying
778. Being surprised on your birthday
779. Learning to express your feelings
780. Being held every night
781. Skiing the Rocky Mountains in Canada
782. Pilates
783. Preparing a dinner party
784. Homemade grilled cheese
785. *The Tudors*
786. Going to a new baseball stadium for the first time
787. Swimming with your significant other
788. Wearing a size 0
789. Renewing your faith
790. Clean, fresh towels
791. Getting phone calls checking in from your significant other
792. Making the dishes your mom used to make
793. Dad always taking care of your car, no matter how old you are
794. Going to a destination wedding
795. Swallowing fear and just doing it
796. Feeling sexy
797. Knowing it's the end of a very long day
798. 5-inch stilettos
799. The steam room
800. Trying out a new dessert recipe
801. Making scrambled eggs in a cast iron skillet
802. Sitting on a bar stool at a bar
803. Running into a friend on the street
804. The first hint of spring

805. Vacuuming
806. *Iron Chef America*
807. Girls night out
808. Finding a heads-up penny just when you need it
809. Ladybugs
810. A caffeine high that lasts for hours
811. An ex-boyfriend spontaneously wants to see you
812. Sundays
813. Hearing waves crash from a distance
814. The plastic clips that keep opened bags closed
815. Bluetooth
816. Laughing at your own jokes
817. The moment after your car is washed
818. Buying fresh flowers at the farmer's market
819. Your favorite black leather jacket that never gets old
820. Working out so hard it hurts
821. Jewelry with sentimental value
822. Getting hit on at a restaurant when you weren't even trying
823. Breathing
824. Being held at night
825. Being held in the morning
826. Slightly chilled cheesecake
827. Allowing a car to merge in front of you
828. A car allowing you to merge
829. Pet adoption day at the pet store
830. *Homeland*
831. Making plans for the holidays
832. The sound of a wine bottle opening
833. Paying your bills online
834. Listening to a friend tell a story
835. Watching CNN on weekend mornings

836. The smell of freshly brewed coffee
837. All-night diners
838. Resorts that overlook the ocean
839. Valet parking
840. The button on your car trunk that automatically closes it
841. Kindness
842. A brand new blade in your razor
843. A naked baby on the beach
844. Your neighborhood restaurant where everyone knows you
845. Finishing a book
846. Reading the *New York Times* on Sundays
847. Selling some of your old clothes
848. Outdoor concerts with a picnic
849. A stocked fridge
850. Brand new underwear
851. Cats
852. The imprint your foot makes on vacuumed carpet
853. Finally organizing your papers
854. The drive-thru window
855. Making pancakes at home
856. Yoga
857. Still reading books while everyone else is reading on a Kindle
858. Testing out new recipes
859. Finally making that trip to Goodwill
860. That hook under a bar to hang your purse
861. Double coupons
862. Fake eyelashes
863. Playing with the pets at the pet store
864. The moment a baked crab roll enters your mouth
865. Starting at the stars from inside an airplane
866. Neighbors inviting you to their BBQ

867. Finding a parking spot right away
868. Getting to work on time
869. Having a meal made for you at home
870. Your pet
871. Grocery shopping
872. Getting it—that aha moment
873. New opportunities
874. Getting your car detailed
875. Fresh basil
876. The revving of a motorcycle engine
877. A new baseball hat
878. Backless dresses
879. Flip flops
880. Fresh yogurt with granola and fresh fruit on top
881. Talking animals in commercials
882. Baby pictures
883. Planning your costume for Halloween
884. Squirrels in trees
885. Using your sick days when you're not sick
886. The dictionary
887. An empty beach on a weekday
888. Tailored clothes to fit you
889. The U.S. Open Tennis Tournament
890. A night at the theater
891. Being able to afford really expensive boots
892. The friendly bagger at the grocery
893. ATMs at the gas pump
894. New gym clothes
895. A Montblanc pen
896. Movies that make me happy: *Beaches*
897. *The Sound of Music*

898. *Look Who's Talking*
899. *Funny Farm*
900. *Fame*
901. *Terms of Endearment*
902. *It's A Wonderful Life*
903. *Rocky I, II, III, IV, V,* and *Rocky Balboa*
904. *Forest Gump*
905. *Sense and Sensibility*
906. *St. Elmo's Fire*
907. *Life of Pi*
908. *Grease*
909. *Wall Street*
910. *The English Patient*
911. *Gone with the Wind*
912. *The Best Exotic Marigold Hotel*
913. *Breakfast at Tiffany's*
914. *Casablanca*
915. *Shakespeare In Love*
916. Paper shredding
917. Cat noises
918. Rebates
919. Making homemade brownies
920. The tingling feeling you get after you sneeze
921. Foot rubs
922. Cold beer
923. Homemade home fries in a skillet
924. Learning to play guitar
925. Sitting in a hot shower
926. The anticipation before your birthday
927. Babies dressed in Halloween costumes
928. Hearing a stranger play the violin from a window

929. Getting in that last push-up
930. The smell of Pine-Sol
931. Getting taken care of when you're sick
932. Warm socks on a cold night
933. FaceTime
934. Rain that lasts for days
935. Binge watching an entire show on Netflix
936. The word touché
937. A perfectly folded shirt
938. Steam that rises from draining pasta
939. An already paid meter
940. The sound of an owl first thing in the morning
941. Knowing anyone is either a car or plane ride away
942. One frozen pizza left in the freezer
943. Lint rollers
944. The shiny stuff that goes on tires
945. The massage you get when a hairdresser puts the conditioner in your hair
946. Driving by McDonald's and smelling the French fries from inside your car
947. Squeezing in a workout at the end of your day
948. Finding a frozen dinner when you thought the kitchen was empty
949. New dishes just out of the bubble wrap
950. Vintage maps
951. Globes
952. Classic literature
953. Corsets
954. A Juliet balcony
955. Don Henley

956. Memorizing a monologue from a movie and reciting it in character
957. 100-degree heat
958. Doing that last rep when you don't think you can possibly do another one
959. Post-it notes
960. Downward-facing dog
961. Getting new Twitter followers
962. Mahogany furniture
963. Statues of a man and a woman in an embrace
964. Surround sound
965. Phone sex
966. Being the girlfriend of a professional athlete and watching them from the stands
967. Hearing someone's life story
968. People "liking" something of yours on Facebook
969. Your grandma's antique wine glasses
970. Pulling back the shades in the morning on the weekend
971. Sconces
972. The kindness and expertise of the Apple support team
973. Business cards
974. The shade of blue only found in Greece
975. Water in a pool that is not cold
976. Getting a complimentary bottle of wine in your hotel room
977. Ultra-soft toilet paper
978. Bookshelves
979. A deer crossing sign
980. No traffic
981. GPS
982. Travel coffee mugs that don't spill
983. Disney movies

984. The room service cart entering your hotel room
985. A three-year-old's laugh
986. Still using a tea kettle to boil water for tea
987. A hot stone massage with over-the-head showers pouring down on you
988. The smell of fresh lemons
989. Taking out your bikinis for a tropical vacation in the middle of winter
990. Carrots and hummus
991. My yoga teacher's voice
992. Going backstage at a Broadway show
993. Sexting
994. Pictures and YouTube videos of baby animals playing
995. The smell when driving by See's Candy factory in Los Angeles
996. Texting with emojis
997. The smell of Sunday morning breakfast coming from your neighbor's house
998. Praying, just in case it really does work
999. Getting to 999 on my Happy list